HUMAN SEXUALITY IN BIBLICAL PERSPECTIVE

HUMAN SEXUALITY IN BIBLICAL PERSPECTIVE

A Study Guide

Edited by

Carrie A. Mast and Gerald J. Mast

Foreword by

Lois Johns Kaufmann

Illustrated by

Jill Steinmetz

Based on a document prepared by the Human Sexuality Task Group of Central District Conference

Loren Johns, chair; Ron Guengerich, Michael Miller, Kiva Nice-Webb, J. Alexander Sider, Regina Shands Stoltzfus

Cascadia

Publishing House
Telford, Pennsylvania

Cascadia Publishing House LLC orders, information, reprint permissions:
contact@cascadiapublishinghouse.com
1-215-723-9125
126 Klingerman Road, Telford PA 18969
www.CascadiaPublishingHouse.com

Human Sexuality in Biblical Perspective
Copyright © 2016 by Cascadia Publishing House
a division of Cascadia Publishing House LLC, Telford, PA
18969

Library of Congress Catalog Number: 2016032359
ISBN 13: 978-1-68027-006-8; **ISBN 10:** 1-68027-006-0
Book design by Cascadia Publishing House
Art coordination and cover design by Alison King; illustrations by
Jill Steinmetz

The paper used in this publication is recycled and meets the
minimum requirements of American National Standard for Information Sciences—Permanence of Paper for Printed Library Materials, ANSI
Z39.48-1984.

Bible quotations are used by permission, all rights reserved and unless
otherwise noted are from *The New Revised Standard Version* of the Bible,
copyright 1989, by the Division of Christian Education of the National
Council of the Churches of Christ in the USA.

Library of Congress Cataloguing-in-Publication Data
Names: Mast, Carrie A., editor.
Title: Human sexuality in biblical perspective : a study guide /
   edited by Carrie A. Mast and Gerald J. Mast ; foreword by Lois Johns
   Kaufmann ; illustrated by Jill Steinmetz.
Description: Telford, Pennsylvania : Cascadia Publishing House, 2016. |
   "Based on a document prepared by the Human Sexuality Task Group
   of Central District Conference: Loren Johns, chair; Ron Guengerich,
   Michael Miller, Kiva Nice-Webb, J. Alexander Sider, Regina Shands
   Stoltzfus." | Includes bibliographical references.
Identifiers: LCCN 2016032359 | ISBN 9781680270068 (5.5 x 8.5"
   trade pbk. : alk. paper) | ISBN 1680270060 (5.5 x 8.5" trade pbk.)
Subjects: LCSH: Sex--Biblical teaching. | Sex--Religious aspects--
   Mennonite Church USA--Textbooks. | Sex--Religious aspects--
   Anabaptists--Textbooks. | Mennonite Church USA--Doctrines. |
   Anabaptists--Doctrines.
Classification: LCC BS680.S5 H86 2016 | DDC 202/.12--dc23
LC record available at https://lccn.loc.gov/2016032359

22 21 20 19 18 17 16   10 9 8 7 6 5 4 3 2 1

CONTENTS

FOREWORD

FOLLOWERS OF JESUS SEEK TO BE FAITHFUL in our love of God and neighbor in response to the love and grace we have received from God. We do so in our personal lives and in our churches. It is in faith communities where we discern the living shape of that faithfulness. In the context of the congregation, love and common purpose can create a healthy setting for the varied paces and pulls of individual growth and growth of the whole.

The inherent and dynamic tension between individual growth and that of the congregation is part of the church's story. As the circle grows from congregation to conference, the dynamic tension can increase. As leaders of a conference with congregations large and small, rural and urban, we have tried to create circles of conversation at our conference gatherings around unity of purpose in the midst of diversity of perspective and pace of change.

As many of our congregations have moved toward full inclusion of gay and lesbian Christian couples, some have also felt called to extend that welcome to the role of pastoral leadership. At the same time, other congregations have continued to follow the traditional teaching that sexual intimacy should be reserved for married heterosexual couples. So we continue to need settings, common language, and biblical tools for our circles of conversation.

Discernment is a slow process aided by earnest commitment to each other and to our common desire to be faithful followers of Jesus Christ. It most logically belongs in the local congregation, where relationships of respect best bear the tension of diversity. Mutual commitment to conference life, with its gifts of shared resources and inspiration, does not require uniformity of belief and practice. But the understanding and care that arise within relationships are essential, lest congregations function in isolation and we lose our commitment to give and receive counsel.

We anticipate that this study guide will serve the congregations of Central District Conference, and perhaps the broader church as well, in continuing the loving dialogue to which our conference committed, along with many other Mennonite conferences, thirty years ago. We did not design this document as a policy statement to be affirmed or rejected but rather as a discussion tool to be tested and questioned. We do, however, believe that this study guide offers a fresh biblical perspective that deserves prayerful consideration and conversation as we welcome the call of God's Spirit to test and discern patterns of faithfulness in our time and place.

—Lois Johns Kaufmann, *Conference Minister of Central District Conference, Ascension Day 2016*

INTRODUCTION

THIS STUDY GUIDE PROVIDES an opportunity to explore biblical understandings of human sexuality, and our stewardship of sexuality, as expressed in two documents released by Central District Conference (CDC), a regional conference of Mennonite Church USA. The first document is a statement made in 2014 by the conference's Ministerial Committee explaining their decision to license a pastor who is a gay man (see Appendix B).

The second document was composed by a task group of the conference charged with creating a new statement that reflects CDC's emerging understandings of sexuality. The document provides biblical and theological reasons for these emerging understandings, which express "faithful dissent" to some traditional teachings about sexuality and marriage and affirm nonconformity to narrow worldly judgments about sexual norms.

These understandings have been displayed in decisions made by many congregations of the conference to more fully include sexually nonconforming people and their families in the life of the church. The conference leadership regards these decisions to be consistent with historic Mennonite commitments to social nonconformity as a practice of Christian discipleship. Thus, in this study guide, we speak of sexual nonconformity as a positive good that challenges the whole church, by the mercies of God, to conform to Jesus Christ rather than to the dividing and excluding patterns of the world (Romans 12:1-2). This commitment to an embracing biblical nonconformity links the discussion of human sexuality in this guide with a range of other topics and experiences, such as family life, sexual abuse, pornography, divorce, violence, biblical interpretation, and more.

Of course, members of the church are not always agreed about how to apply biblical convictions. During the past ten years, CDC conference assemblies have generally affirmed the actions of inclusive congregations and pastors, even while some leaders and congregations in the conference have also raised questions and concerns about this direction. Such questions and concerns have been expressed in a variety of venues: open-mike opportunities at annual meetings, regional gatherings, conversations with our conference minister, letters to the board of directors, and decisions by congregations to withdraw from the conference.

MENNONITE DISCUSSIONS AND DECISIONS

The decisions and discernment of Central District Conference about human sexuality have taken place against the backdrop of its relationships with the network of conferences known as Mennonite Church USA. The process of discussion and discernment about same-sex relationships within that larger network has been unfolding for the past three decades, beginning with developments in the two predecessor denominational bodies: the General Conference Mennonite Church and the Mennonite Church.

In July 1986, the General Conference Mennonite Church met at Saskatoon, Saskatchewan, and passed a resolution on human sexuality that affirmed the goodness of human sexuality, confessed to judgmental attitudes that included the rejection of those with a different sexual orientation, and established a covenant to continue to discern and to remain open to dialogue on these matters. At the same time, the resolution confirmed the church's understanding that sexual intercourse is reserved for a man and woman in marriage. A year later, the (Old) Mennonite Church made a similar resolution at their assembly at Purdue University in West Lafayette, Indiana.

Since the 1980s, the Saskatoon and Purdue statements, along with *Human Sexuality in the Christian Life*, published in 1985 as the official church study guide on this topic, have served as landmarks in the discussion of human sexuality in the Mennonite churches. Most official statements of Mennonite churches, conferences, and other bodies have reflected their commitment to heterosexual marriage while becoming more explicit about their condemnation of same-sex unions or marriages. The 1995 *Confession of Faith in a Mennonite Perspective*, which established the doctrinal unity upon which Mennonite Church USA was formed in 2002, stated in article 19 that "we believe that God intends marriage to be a covenant between one man and one woman for life."

Meanwhile, convictions and perspectives on human sexuality have continued to change in the church as relationships that do not conform to traditional heterosexual marriage are blessed by some congregations and bear good fruit. Some see this change as a clear departure from faithfulness and from the Bible while some see it as evidence of the Holy Spirit's direction toward a more inclusive and embracing church. Others see it as a call into an unspoken liminal or in-between space marked by love for others without a clear sense of how this in-between space lines up with biblical and theological values.

Liminal space like this has been part of the church's experience during changing perspectives on most issues, whether it is the wearing of a prayer veiling or the acceptability of divorce and remarriage. In such cases the church has not typically worked out an acceptable theology before changing its practice but rather searched the Scriptures for wisdom about how to address challenges that were already changing the church.

For example, growing discomfort with slavery in the nineteenth century led the church to read the Bible in new ways, seeing for the first time the prophetic challenge to human enslavement and the jubilee promise of liberation that was there all along. Just as theology is a matter of faith seeking understanding, so is ethics often a matter of changing practice and new awareness seeking biblical and theological footing.

During the thirty years since the Saskatoon and Purdue statements, the church (like the surrounding society) has been faced with new challenges and insights concerning sexuality, especially focusing on concerns involving same-sex relationships. More broadly, the issues of sexual relationships and intimacy outside of marriage—for single persons of all ages—have confronted both society and congregations. None of these concerns is likely to disappear, and the church has not found consistent and helpful responses to these questions either by ignoring the concerns or by uncritically restating what has been said in the past.

Neither, however, is the church well served by simply dismissing traditional wisdom. Instead, this situation calls on us as followers of Jesus to return to the source of all wisdom and to examine the scriptures again in light of the way

Jesus responded to and talked about human relationships (at least implicitly including sexuality).

In the Anabaptist tradition, discernment about faithful Christian discipleship takes place in congregational discussion and decisions, as well as in exchanges of counsel among congregations and church leaders within the broader network of the conference. Consistent with these commitments, the Saskatoon and Purdue resolutions of 1986 and 1987 established a covenant for Mennonites to

> mutually bear the burden of remaining in loving dialogue with each other in the body of Christ, recognizing that we are all sinners in need of God's grace and that the Holy Spirit may lead us to further truth and repentance.

TESTING AND CONFIRMING DIRECTION

As noted earlier, this guide displays the counsel represented in two documents produced through various discernment processes in CDC: 1) "Theological Foundations for Credentialing" (see Appendix B); and 2) "Human Sexuality: A Biblical Perspective." The study guide offers this counsel in a format and style suited to study and discussion within a variety of settings and formats as described in Appendix A.

Most of the content of the second document is included throughout this study guide, even though the content is organized somewhat differently and a substantial amount of new material has been added. The exact text of the original "Human Sexuality: A Biblical Perspective" document may be found at the CDC website located at the following URL: *http://www.mcusacdc.org/resources/conference-documents/.*

With prayer for the Holy Spirit's guidance, we offer this study guide as one way to test the direction the CDC is moving. Many voices have contributed to this project: the ministerial committee, the human sexuality task group, the editors, the illustrator, the designer, the publisher, the conference leadership, and a host of additional voices from our conference both affirming and critical.

Earlier drafts of the guide have been tested in regional conference gatherings, in congregational Christian education classes, and with conference pastors and teachers. These discussions have led to substantial revisions to the study guide, including greater attention to biblical texts that seem to address same-sex attraction, clear confrontation of violence and abuse in sexually intimate relationships (whether outside of or in marriage), and more clarity about the approach to biblical discernment displayed here.

We are grateful for all of these voices that have contributed through an Anabaptist process of giving and receiving counsel to bring this study guide to fruition. The final text should not be regarded as a consensus document since it is unlikely that any person involved in the process (including the editors!) agrees perfectly with every single sentence or statement. Instead the text of the study guide should be regarded as a snapshot of a discernment process by one group of God's people who are walking together on the road of discipleship.

For the CDC, the covenant to dialogue expressed in the Saskatoon and Purdue resolutions has led us during the past thirty years to "further truth and repentance" as represented in the theological and practical understandings displayed in this study guide. We have experienced the presence and confirmation of the Holy Spirit in our discussions and decisions, even when these discussions have included disagreement. Perhaps most profoundly, we have experienced the great joy of reconciliation as our conference has extended the hand of fellowship to brothers and sisters in Christ from whom we had at one time been alienated because of previous judgments made by conference and denominational bodies.

We are grateful for those whose voices and lives have helped us to discover the wideness of God's mercy. We are also thankful for those whose persistent questions and challenges have helped us to remain accountable to the wisdom of tradition. We commend the knowledge we have discovered in our brotherly and sisterly conversations to the church for further testing and confirmation—as well as for the moral and spiritual guidance we have found in our study of the Bible during changing times.

HUMAN SEXUALITY
IN BIBLICAL
PERSPECTIVE

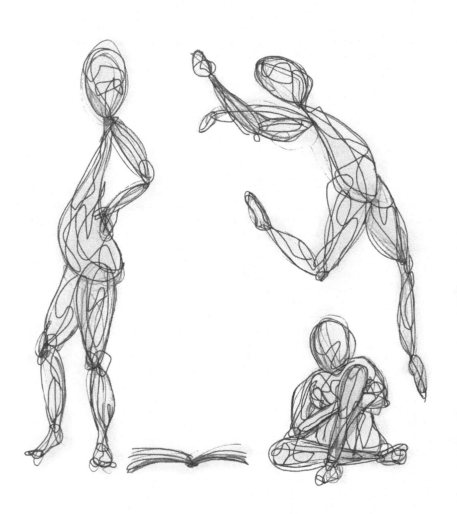

one

OUR BODIES AND THE BIBLE

Chapter 1

OUR BODIES AND THE BIBLE

IN THE ANABAPTIST TRADITION, we ordinarily begin our discernment about faithful discipleship with the witness of Scripture to the Word of God. "What does the Bible say about this?" we ask. "What does Jesus teach us about that?" we continue. At the same time, we cannot help but bring our experience as living and breathing creatures to our understanding of the Bible.

With regard to sexuality, we know that our orientation to the world and to other people is part of this experience. What we love and desire shapes what we know and believe. It is good to acknowledge these life experiences and perspectives when we study the Bible together for greater understanding of God's will.

GOOD BODIES

As Anabaptist Christians, we believe that God's creation is good, even if broken, and that therefore we ourselves are the good work of God's hands. Though sin and failure compromise our humanity, God affirms humanity to be one of the good works of creation (Gen. 1:31). Because of this goodness in our creatureliness, what we see and experience of the physical world around us, including our own bodies, can be understood as part of what early Anabaptist writers like Hans Hut called the "book of creation" or the "gospel of the creatures" through which God speaks to us (123-25). The heavens are telling the glory of God, the Psalmist says, and human beings are crowned with God's glory and honor (Ps. 19:1; 8:5).

Because God's creation is good and because it communicates the goodness and purposes of God to us, we should acknowledge that our perception of the creation through our bodily experiences is a part of our knowledge of God. This bodily knowledge includes our experience of being male and female or of not easily fitting into one of these categories. This knowledge also includes our experiences of attraction and desire.

All of this is to say that we come to understand God's love partly through our own embodied and engendered experiences of human love; we understand God's desire partly through human desire. This knowledge is described by theologian Melanie May as "revelatory presence" (108). Such knowledge through creation incorporates our experiences of loving and of being loved, including experiences of sexual desire and intimacy.

For example, our desire for friendship and relationship with one another helps us to understand God's desire for friendship and relationship. Our experience of alienation and betrayal helps us to understand God's experience of alienation and betrayal. Our experience of family life helps us to understand God's experience of God's family. The book of Hosea in the Bible testifies vividly to this correlation between human intimacy and its betrayal on the one hand, and God's love for God's people and their betrayal of that love, on the other hand.

These experiences of love and desire and inhabiting bodies are a part of the truth that God reveals to us in the creation. Knowing ourselves and loving others helps us to know and to love God.

These experiences of love and desire also shape how we read and interpret what the Bible tells us about the nature and will of God and in particular how we understand the meaning of the birth, life, death, and resurrection of Jesus Christ. Bringing our lives into relationship with the life of Jesus Christ as displayed in scripture is what it means to be a disciple of Jesus Christ. From Jesus we learn about what it means to be fully human in both mind and body.

BROKEN BODIES

Even as we experience the delight of human love and intimacy, we also find that our desires are subject to corruption and abuse. This knowledge of human brokenness that is so often discovered in the failures of friendship and the abuses of intimacy is knowledge that can wound and scar our humanity, affecting our capacity for giving and receiving love and altering our experience of desire and attachment. Such experiences of hurt and harm also contribute to our knowledge of God, who suffers with us and identifies with our pain and sorrow, having been afflicted just as we are, to the extent of betrayal by his friends and crucifixion on a cross (Heb. 4:15).

Thus, we recognize that being human includes the bodily knowledge of love's birth as well as love's betrayal. We have learned of the creation's goodness in our bodily experiences and felt the fall in our relationship failures.

We have also experienced brokenness when the distinctive and God-created goodness of our human bodies and holy desires are denied by our communities and fam-

ilies. When those who are close to us tell us that our bodies
or our desires are unwelcome as God created them, then
the very image of God has been rejected in the name of an
unholy and idolatrous human image. Such rejection of the
image of God in us and in our neighbors is at the root of so
much of the violence and abuse that is tragically present in
human relationships.

CHURCH BODIES

Because of human brokenness and the limits of our individual bodies, we cannot rely only on our personal experience as the basis for understanding God's will and
purpose. As human beings made in the image of God, we
have capacities for reasoning and analysis that allow us to
empathize with the experiences of others who are different from us and that permit us to develop perspectives on
the world that account for more than our own sight and
awareness.

This need that we have to account for the experiences
and understandings of others leads to an essential practice
of life in the church—giving and receiving of counsel. In
giving and receiving counsel we listen to the perspectives
and experiences of other believers and we share our own
perspectives and experiences—not as an expression of
judgment but as a display of partnership and support in
our common search to follow Jesus faithfully. Through
this experience of life together, we are able to go beyond a
merely human point of view to glimpse the life of the new
and reconciled creation that God is bringing about
through the life, death, and resurrection of Jesus Christ (2
Cor. 5:16-18).

The apostle Paul describes this community of sharing
and learning that is brought together in Jesus Christ as a
communal body: one with many members and distinctive

gifts. This church body is made of many human bodies that are transformed by their attachment to one another through baptism into the church body. When one member of this body suffers, all suffer. If one member is honored, all rejoice. The least member is honored the most. Every gift of knowledge, whether of prophecy, teaching, leadership, interpretation, or cross-cultural communication, is received as necessary for the thriving of the body (1 Cor. 12).

At the center of this church body's sharing and discernment is the Word of God as given in Scripture. The Bible provides us with the defining key to the correction of our own limited and broken experiences of the world through our bodies.

In the Bible we find a story that is larger than our own lives, wisdom that exceeds our own common sense, admonitions to repentance from our iniquities and sins, and visions of hope for a coming world of peace and restored relationships. When read and absorbed together with our brothers and sisters in Christ in the presence of the Holy Spirit, the Bible is a reliable guide to the solid ground of God's Word and a vital resource for the truthful interpretation of God's creation.

STUDY QUESTIONS

1. What difference will it make for discussions about sexuality to include participants in the discussion who express differing bodily experiences: married, single, young, gay, elderly, bisexual, straight, disabled, white, etc.?

2. How does betrayal affect our understandings of love and intimacy?

3. What role does listening play in receiving the gifts of the body of Christ, the church?

4. How can we make sure to grant the Bible a defining voice in our discernment as a body of Christ? What con-

tributes to honoring the voice of scripture and what contributes to blocking this voice in our processes of discernment?

5. In what ways do the "book of creation" and the "gospel of the creatures" speak to us today? How does the natural world, including scientific knowledge about this world, help us to know God's will in our own time and place?

6. How does the visual illustration at the beginning of this chapter express the relationships between human bodies and the Bible?

7. With which of the bodies in this chapter's opening visual illustration do you most identify? Why?

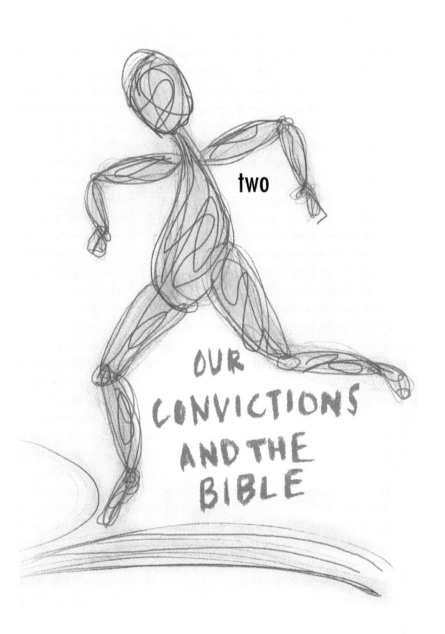

two

OUR
CONVICTIONS
AND THE
BIBLE

Chapter 2

OUR CONVICTIONS AND THE BIBLE

As WE BRING OUR BODILY EXPERIENCES into conversation with the Bible and with one another, we begin to have a better understanding about who God is and what God wants. This picture of God helps us to know who we are as human beings created in God's image. As a result we get more clarity about our Christian calling and how it relates to the practices of our lives.

As we seek to bring our lives—including our bodily experiences—into the light of the Scriptures, we acknowledge with the writer of 2 Timothy that "all Scripture is inspired by God and is useful for teaching, for reproof, for correction, and for training in righteousness, so that everyone who belongs to God may be proficient, equipped for every good work" (3:16-17). This commitment to attend to "all Scripture" and not only to a proof text here or there that supports what we already believe helps us to listen to the Bible rather than to use it as a trump card in church conflict.

By "all Scripture," of course, we mean the writings associated with the Hebrew Bible, to which the writer of 2 Timothy was likely referring, as well as the writings canonized as the "New Testament" by the Christian church. For our purposes, we accept the principle articulated in 2 Timothy 3 to apply to all of the scriptures accepted as canonical by the church, even though the writer of 2 Timothy could not have been referring to the as yet uncanonized "New Testament" writings.

DIFFERENCE IN THE BIBLE

When we attend to "all Scripture," we discover that the Bible is itself a community of difference and argument rather than a consistent and seamless answer book. It is a book that challenges and stretches our faith by not always behaving itself; that is, by exceeding our expectations (Enns 9). Paul Hanson has explained that when we acknowledge this diversity of points of view found in the Bible, we can experience the Bible as disclosing a "living relationship" rather than a fossilized record of "infallible doctrines" (2).

We realize, for instance, that the Bible had multiple human authors who wrote and spoke from different perspectives in at least three different ancient languages— Hebrew, Aramaic, and Greek—across a span of a thousand-plus years. Early Anabaptist writers like Balthasar Hubmaier and Hans Denck highlight these differences in the Bible by publishing lists of contradictory passages in the Bible and insisting that a truthful interpretation needs to account for contrasting perspectives as readers seek to respond to wisdom of the Holy Spirit that surpasses any individual's wisdom. Hubmaier writes that unless these contrasting perspectives are acknowledged and addressed, the result will be a "half truth" that is "more damaging than a whole lie" and that leads to the extinguishing of brotherly and sisterly love (428).

As a document, the Bible is not an unchanging text. For example, in the centuries following the birth of the church, Christianity expanded the canon of the Hebrew Bible used by Jesus to include the New Testament books. During the Protestant Reformation, scripture scholars debated the status of books sometimes regarded as apocryphal that were included in the Latin Vulgate Bible such as 1 and 2 Maccabees and Tobit. The result of this argument is that most Protestant Bibles no longer include the Apocrypha, whereas these books continue to be part of Catholic Bibles. Beyond such dramatic changes in the scripture canon, textual scholars who examine the manuscript tradition continually assess and revise our assumptions about the specific wording of the most reliably established text of a particular passage. Every time a new translation of the Bible is published, it undergoes change at the basic level of what words appear in it and in what order.

Given these and a host of other factors, contemporary Christians should not be surprised that Christian interpretations of Scripture change over time with changes in language, setting, and audience. When Christians develop a theology of Scripture, they need to pay special attention to how these factors shape their imaginations about what Scripture is and how it functions in the life of faith. We should certainly consider such matters as change in setting and audience as we develop a theology of Scripture with regard to human sexuality and gender identity.

When we can identify contrasting perspectives within the Bible, we see that some of those perspectives belonged to people who lived on the margins of their societies. For example, feminist Bible scholar Phyllis Trible has helped us to see that even biblical texts that appear to align God with male patriarchs such as Abraham also attend to the experiences and traumas of women, like Abraham's wife Sarah who he betrayed and his slave Hagar, whom he abused and dismissed (*Texts* 9-35). It has long been noticed that the Evangelist Luke seems to have paid special attention to people who were poor or sick in his portrayal of the gospel story (Moxnes 52-55).

More recently, scholars have suggested that numerous texts from both the Old and New Testaments contain evidence of having been written from marginalized Jewish perspectives. Many of the Old Testament scriptures, for example, appear to have been written or compiled to address the trauma of Jewish deportation to Babylon in the sixth century B.C.E. (Smith Christopher 54-73.).

In the first three Gospels, Jesus is portrayed as a Jew from Galilee, not Judea. Hence he represents a kind of Judaism that does not conform to the perspectives of the powerful Jewish authorities associated with the Jerusalem temple. Jesus' challenge to temple-centered piety develops an upside-down and inside-out display of the in-breaking kingdom of God that replaces "the machinery of formalized religion with compassion and love" (Kraybill 69).

JESUS IN THE BIBLE

The teachings and actions of Jesus as depicted in the first four books of the New Testament confirm the biblical concern for people on the margins of society. Recognizing that many persons who identify as sexual and gender minorities today feel marginalized in their own lives and communities (including church communities), we believe that Christians who follow Jesus should look at how Jesus related to those who were marginalized or nonconforming in the first century.

Jesus himself was sexually and/or gender nonconforming in a number of ways. First, as Brittany E. Wilson has pointed out, Jesus displayed many characteristics that were considered "unmanly" according to the controlling masculinity of the ancient world and perhaps in our world too (190-242). His ministry identified with the weak and the sick (Mark 2:17); he wept in public on a variety of occasions (Luke 19:41; John 11:35); he spent an unusual amount of time in thoughtful conversation with women—allowing himself to be corrected by a woman in at least one context (Matt. 15:22-28)—and he gave himself up to his enemies rather than fight them with the sword (Matt. 26:47-56).

Second, Jesus was sexually nonconforming in his singleness, given that Jewish men of his age usually married. Instead of living in a heterosexual relationship as a husband with a wife and as a father of children, he spent most of his adult life with a small group of friends and disciples whom he came to regard as his family, "my brother and sister and mother" (Matt. 12:46-50). This circle of beloved friends was the primary context in which Jesus expressed and experienced the intimacy of shared food, conversation, and emotional support.

Jesus' interactions with women did not conform to the gender segregated public culture of ancient Palestine. For example, his conversation with the Samaritan woman is instructive as we notice how he related to this woman who was clearly outside the "circle of the righteous," as defined by the Jerusalem norms (John 4). Because of the ways in which she was labeled—woman, Samaritan, divorced, living with someone not her husband—this woman would have been easily dismissed within the patriarchal world of Jerusalem and quite possibly by many in the church today.

But Jesus did not slide into such prejudice and judgment. Instead, knowing all this, Jesus discussed theology with her—the spiritual meaning of water and eternal life, the proper location and focus of worship, and the power of messianic hope. During this intriguing, respectful, empowering, and theologically rich conversation with the woman from Samaria, Jesus did not mention condemnation nor did he call for her to repent.

Jesus' relationships with other women also reflected healthy, righteous, and compassionate relationships and sexuality. The intimacy Jesus "allowed" was shocking to many around him: talking with the Samaritan woman, affirming the woman who touched him and massaged his feet as she anointed him, refusing to condemn and enter judgment on an adulterous woman, delighting in Mary (Martha's sister) who wanted to listen to his teaching, and showing concern for a widow whose son had died, for a girl who was sick and had died, for sisters who were grieving for (and perhaps dependent on) a brother who had died.

The regularity of such interactions in Jesus' social practice paints a picture of respectful and attentive human intimacy that for Jesus was much more than a matter of anatomy and biology or of fulfilling desires. In the New Testament examples above and elsewhere, we see Jesus relating to others in ways that focused on building life-giving relationships; he did not reduce people to their sexuality or gender identity nor did he make intimacy about sexual conquest. Instead, through his practices of fellowship and healing, he showed that the life and beauty of human bodies are an integral part of our whole human experience and of how we see our places in the world.

This life and beauty is given but not taken in Jesus' relationships. Moreover, Jesus teaches that building life-affirming relationships begins with an attitude of respect. For instance, adultery as Jesus defines it is more than a genital activity; it is a sinful way of seeing another person that is called lust (Matt. 5:27-28).

RELATIONSHIPS IN THE BIBLE

The Bible describes a variety of social contexts in which sexual intimacy occurs. Some intimate relationships appear to be loving and fulfilling (Isaac and Rebekah) while others are clearly abusive and adulterous (David and Bathsheba). The Bible depicts incestuous sexual encounters—between parents and children (Lot and his daughters) and between brothers and sisters (Tamar and Amnon).

Other accounts depict sex between married persons (Rachel and Jacob and also Leah and Jacob), between male householders and female servants (Abraham and Hagar), between unmarried people who become married (Ruth and Boaz), between unmarried lovers who remain unmarried (Song of Songs), between a prophet and a prostitute (Hosea), between a king and his harem (Solomon and his seven hundred wives and three hundred concubines)—and the list goes on.

A number of same-sex relationships in the Bible display profound attachment and covenant love, even if not necessarily sexual intimacy, between two men (David and Jonathan) and between two women (Ruth and Naomi).

Sometimes accounts of these relationships include moral judgment; other times not. Marriage relationships are sometimes monogamous and sometimes polygamous. Sometimes the description of sexual intimacy—such as is found in the Song of Songs—implies that sexuality is an intrinsic good. At other times sexual desire is shown to be a result of sin—Eve's desire for her husband after the Fall (Gen. 3:16). Some intimate relationships are shown to be casual and dysfunctional romances, such as Samson and Delilah, while others are based in exclusive covenants such as between David and Jonathan.

The same diversity of relationship practices is displayed in connection with other ethical choices described in the Bible, including various approaches to dealing with enemies, for example. Throughout the Bible, people respond to enemies in a variety of ways: killing them, taking them as slaves, exiling them, stoning them, praying for their misfortune, forgiving them, sparing their lives, being reconciled to them. Some passages of Scripture assume that destroying enemies is a command of God (Deut. 7:2); some passages assert that killing is forbidden (Deut. 5:17).

Rarely do we find that there are fixed forms for our lives and relationships prescribed in the biblical texts. Rather, we find persuasive stories of people struggling with sin and of God's unwavering desire to restore humanity through the obedience of faith.

As Christians, we believe that Jesus Christ is the fullest expression of God's desire to redeem our humanity and so we turn to Jesus in order to know how to respond to the human condition as truthfully described in the Bible. Thus, interpreting Scripture has to do with "reading" the many contexts in which Christians today live their daily lives in the light of Jesus' life and teachings.

Just as in the scriptures he taught and discussed, Jesus does not prescribe fixed forms or unalterable rules to follow for how we are to relate to people. He does, however, prescribe faithful habits and practices that display the loving righteousness of God. These are the practices that should guide our relationship choices: love your enemies; do not judge; keep your promises; let your yes be yes and your no, no, and more (Matt. 5, 6, and 7). Jesus summarizes all of these practices of God's righteousness by restating the "greatest commandment" from Deuteronomy 6:5: "You shall love the Lord your God with all your heart, with all your soul, and with all your mind," and then Jesus adds "a second which is like it; you shall love your neighbor as yourself" (Matt. 22:36-40).

As we read the gospel stories, we see Jesus as someone

concerned with how people treat each other and with the attitudes they bring to their interpersonal encounters with enemies and lovers alike. In other words, the focus is on how people express love for God and neighbor.

This love for both God and neighbor guides the way Jesus applies and adapts rules—even good rules. For example, Jesus is willing technically to break good rules that require rest on the Sabbath day in order to heal the man with a withered hand because of course it is "lawful to do good on the Sabbath" (Matt. 12:12). For Jesus, doing what is good and loving is more important than doing what is legal and correct.

Jesus calls us to love our enemies. In different situations, this practice takes different forms, sometimes involving loving confrontation and at other times thoughtful tolerance. Jesus calls us to be faithful to the relationships we establish (as we noticed above, committing adultery can be a matter of the heart). In different situations, this practice, too, will take different forms and be applied in a variety of ways.

As we respond to our neighbors with the love of Christ, we display what we have learned through the peaceable life, merciful teachings, passionate death, and reconciling resurrection of Jesus. In the perfection of Christ we have been shown what God desires for us. The light of Jesus Christ shines in the Bible as the most profound meaning of scripture—a way of peace and justice and embrace that goes "beyond the law" to transcend all the violence and domination and exclusion recorded in scripture (Clemens 35-48). We seek therefore to read scripture as Jesus did in his life and teachings.

CHANGE IN THE BIBLE

Christians interpret Scripture as addressing us and implying a vocation—a way of life. We believe that Jesus calls us: "Learn from me." This calling includes learning to interpret as he interpreted Scripture. Jesus models a *dynamic reading* of the Law and the Prophets (the Old Testament). By "dynamic reading" we mean that Jesus understands the interpretation and application of Scripture to change over time and in response to new circumstances.

Perhaps this dynamic reading is most dramatically demonstrated in Jesus' response to the Syrophoenician woman referenced earlier in this chapter. Since she is a Gentile outsider, Jesus initially dismisses her appeal for him to cast a demon out of her daughter (Mark 7:24-30). Jesus' position has valid scriptural grounding; in Matthew's version of the story Jesus interprets the Hebrew prophets in an exclusive, rather than inclusive, way: "I was sent only to the lost sheep of the house of Israel" (Matt. 15:24).

Jesus uses a negative metaphor to interpret the meaning of his own mission in light of scripture: "It is not fair to take the children's food and throw it to the dogs" (Matt. 15:26). But the Syrophoenician woman challenges Jesus with a brilliant rhetorical comeback: "Yes, Lord, yet even the dogs eat the crumbs that fall from their master's table" (Matt. 15:27). As Mennonite pastor Mark Rupp has pointed out, Jesus responds to the Syrophoenician woman's appeal by changing his mind. Jesus commends the woman for her great faith and heals her daughter.

Jesus' dynamic interpretation of Scripture is also seen in his extended teaching in Matthew 5, where he addresses a series of readings of the Old Testament. Jesus affirms the importance of the Old Testament while also bringing a new perspective to this foundational text. Six times he emphasizes, *"You have heard it was said, but I say to you. . . ."* If we learn from Jesus, we will examine the Scriptures in the spirit of Jesus' approach to explaining the Bible, assuming that there is a conventional understanding of what the Bible says—"you have heard it said"—as well as a gospel perspective—"but I say to you." This way of reading the Old Testament as Jesus modeled needs to be part of how we read the texts that appear to deal with same-sex relationships and other "nonconforming" sexualities.

We suggest that an appropriate theology of Scripture leads to the practice of dynamic reading. Such reading keeps in mind the statement by the author of 2 Timothy that "all Scripture is profitable." It is this commitment to "all Scripture" that both perplexes and calls us to continually return to Scripture, asking the question, "What else does Scripture have to say (in light of Jesus) that gives us further perspective on how we practice the love of Christ in all our relationships?" We trust that when we seek God's will through the study of Scripture we will find that the good news of the gospel is even better and more embracing than we had realized.

Study Questions

1. What are some examples of poor interpretations of the Bible based on only a single passage?

2. Why can it be hard to notice the obvious differences of perspective and conviction displayed in the Bible? Why, for example, is it easy to ignore that in the same book there is both a rule against killing and a command to kill?

3. What does it mean for privileged people to stand with Jesus on the margins in the way we make decisions about human relationships?

4. What are some examples of changing interpretations of the Bible in the Christian church and in the Mennonite church?

5. What are some examples of commitments and convictions that appear to have been unchanged over time in the Christian church and the Mennonite church?

6. What are two different ways of being grounded in Scripture that are displayed in the visual illustration at the beginning of this chapter?

7. With which of the figures in the visual illustration at the beginning of this chapter do you most identify? Why?

three

SEXUALITY IN THE BIBLE: OLD TESTAMENT

Chapter 3

SEXUALITY IN THE BIBLE: OLD TESTAMENT

WHEN WE INTERPRET SCRIPTURE DYNAMICALLY, keeping in mind both similarities and differences within it, we can discern fuller pictures of human sexuality and gender identity than we can when we approach the Bible as primarily a rulebook that has a clearly circumscribed list of texts pertaining to human sexuality. Taking this approach also means that we are able to listen to the whole of Scripture, rather than only to those passages that conform to our assumptions about what the Bible says.

In the following few paragraphs, we look at several passages from the Old Testament that address gender and sexuality and we consider how these passages inform our faith when we read them dynamically. This means that as we interpret the meaning of these passages we strive to understand not only what a passage appears to say in its setting but also how these passages are understood by later Old Testament texts, by New Testament writers, and especially by Jesus.

GENESIS 1 AND 2

In the beginning, God made males and females as relational and biological partners. The creation accounts in Genesis 1 and 2 offer a radical perspective on the relationship of females and males—a perspective often ignored, misread, or forgotten. Indeed, several thought-provoking and striking statements paint a picture of the world that God desired, intended, and called "good." Much of this picture challenges the social norms of patriarchy and related systems of domination that we continue to experience in our world today.

In Genesis 1, male and female are created in the image of God. They are given the blessing that commissions them to "be fruitful and multiply and fill the earth, and subdue it and have dominion over it." What is lost in the English translations of this narrative is that the blessing is a plural imperative given to both males and females. Dominion is to be shared (Trible, *Rhetoric* 20-21). The blessing, understood in this way, would give us the radical thrust of this commission: "*You all,* be fruitful and multiply, and *you all,* have dominion."

From the beginning, both sexes were created together. Biblical scholarship has helped Christians acknowledge that the mandate to share in responsibility for the created world was nonhierarchical. Genesis 1 and 2 highlight intentional mutuality that is *original* but is broken and disrupted when the humans act out of self-interest, ignoring the community and fellowship with each other that God had mandated (Roop 46).

This mandate for mutuality and interdependence stands in stark contrast to the male-dominant individualism and independence that marks our world and that people of privilege exercise *over* those whom they see as *subservient* to themselves. Indeed, as Menno Simons confirmed in his writings, Genesis 1 and 2 treat male domination and female subordination as the *result* of sin and the fall rather than an expression of God's order in creation (113).

Both Jesus and Paul pick up on this motif of mutuality and interdependence and expect "the kingdom" to take this shape, as we will see in the next chapter. It is significant that in this first creation narrative, the creation of male and female in the image of God is not linked specifically to the marriage covenant. The original created state of males and females is as single, not married. Here sexual difference is simply seen as a remarkable part of God's flourishing and diverse creation—a dimension of humanity that reflects the image of God.

The second creation narrative in Genesis 2 is just as informative and intriguing as the first one. God acknowledges after the creation of the first, single, and solitary human that, "it is not good that this human should be alone" (v. 18). The implications of this comment should not be overlooked in our context. A human being that is without companionship or community is, therefore, lacking in a basic component of health and life.

What is the answer to this problem of loneliness in the biblical stories? In Genesis 2, the answer is that God creates a partner for Adam, which leads to a family, which becomes a tribe, and to the population of the world by many human families and tribes. In other words, the biblical answer to the problem of loneliness is community.

Of course, when we focus only on Adam and Eve and their children, it seems as if the main form of biblical community is the human family. But here it is helpful to look forward to the New Testament as part of our dynamic reading of the Bible.

Reading the New Testament, we know that the reign of God Jesus Christ proclaimed and embodied becomes the place where human "aloneness" is remedied. In its display of this peaceable reign of God, the church represents God's creation of a home for those who are "alone" in our world. This includes the never married, the widow and widower, the divorced, and those who have no desire for a traditional marriage relationship. It also includes those whose marriage or family relationships fail to fully address the deep loneliness that is often part of the human condition.

By contrast with common understandings of Genesis 2, Jesus and Paul do not focus on the family as the remedy for aloneness. Instead, they focus on the fellowship of following Jesus together as the place in which companionship is both intimate and life-giving. Without condemning families in general, both Jesus and Paul were, in different ways, highly critical of the exclusive loyalties of first-century household structures and advocated for the people of God as an alternative family structure (cf. Matt. 12:46-50; 19:12; Mark 3:31-35; Luke 8:19-21; 11:27-28; John 19:25-27: 1 Cor. 7; Gal. 3:28).

Having examined briefly the New Testament answer to the problem of "aloneness," we come back to Genesis 2, where the dilemma of "aloneness" is resolved by the creation of a partner—a helper. The animals—God's first attempt at finding a suitable complement for the solitary human—are not adequate for the needs of a partner.

The word *helper* for what is needed is translated from the Hebrew term *'ezer*. In the Old Testament, this term refers most frequently to God rather than to other humans. The *'ezer* is not a subordinate, a flunky, a go-fer, or a servant. Instead the *'ezer* is one who can be turned to for help, assistance, and partnership in the addressing of life situations (Roop 323-24).

Looking ahead again to the New Testament, we notice that the entire letter to the Ephesians may be seen as an extended midrash (interpretation or commentary) on these creation accounts. The second creation narrative receives its fulfillment in the "new creation" that the writer of Ephesians expects to be realized in the body of Christ where all persons understand their own needy situations and look to other members for "help" as companions and partners. Indeed, in many of his early letters, the apostle Paul shows how the faith community rather than the family is the context in which human beings find their most basic relationships with others.

So when we take the long view of the salvation story that unfolds throughout the Bible, the culmination of the narrative in Genesis 2 is not the creation of a suitable partner for the solitary human—but in the new math. What follows the division of the "one becoming two" (male and female) is the unifying of "the two become one."

We have been taught to read this second creation narrative to legislate the marriage of one man to one woman as the exclusive way to fulfill this intention of God. The writer of Ephesians did not take this passage that way. There "the two becoming one" is the model for what happens as Jesus breaks down the walls that divided Jew and Gentile and, by extension, male and female, slave and free, and all other persons that were marginalized, excluded, or considered inferior or "outsiders." (Eph. 2: 15-16).

This "two becoming one" as found in Genesis 1:27 appears to align human difference, as exemplified by male and female, with the "image of God." The implication of this alignment has long been debated. Karl Barth maintained that the image of God is expressed in the very relationality of human beings; that is, the need of human beings for companionship and community (184-86). Sarah Coakley has updated Barth's argument by claiming that the desire unleashed in God's creation is "more fundamental than gender" and that therefore desire is "the precious clue woven into the crooked human heart that ever reminds it of its relatedness and its source" (58-59).

Such accounts of the meaning and purpose of human desire for intimacy are part of a long-standing debate in the church about the ultimate meaning of companionship and intimate attachment described in Genesis 2. For example, Christians have explained the meaning and purpose of marriage covenants in sometimes contrasting ways.

The Catholic tradition has placed a higher value on the essential connection between an unalterable marriage relationship and the bearing of children, thus condemning the use of birth control as well as divorce and remarriage, while making openness to children an intrinsic feature of the marriage covenant. On the other hand, the Protestant traditions have generally placed a higher value on covenant love and intimacy, allowing for the use of birth control, as well as the possibility of divorce and remarriage, in the service of healthy relationships of love and intimacy.

Some Protestant traditions have suggested that the church's blessing on unions or marriages between persons of the same sex is in keeping with this valuing of love and intimacy in exclusive relationships. From such a perspective, love, commitment, and intimacy constitute the marriage covenant rather than biological complementarity or procreation. The committee that authored the 1985 book *Human Sexuality in the Christian Life* on behalf of the General Conference Mennonite Church and the Mennonite Church acknowledged the possibility of same-sex covenants but could not reach agreement on whether they could be considered valid (116).

As J. C. Wenger has documented, early Anabaptist writers generally followed Protestant views about marriage more closely, while later Mennonite thinking—especially with respect to questions of divorce and remarriage—reflected the more traditional Catholic view (11-20). In recent times, Mennonites have often borrowed from both Catholic and Protestant thinking in defining marriage in relationship to family life and procreation, especially as conflict has challenged the church in this area.

Apart from the contested question of same-sex marriage, theological exploration on this front has implications for marriages between persons who are infertile or who decide not to have children. In *Human Sexuality in the Christian Life*, the writers affirm that marriages have covenantal value "even when no children are born," and that therefore it is appropriate to "enter into a union for the sake of the covenantal and relational values themselves" (115).

Confirming the intrinsic covenantal worth of marriage, we have seen that in the second creation narrative in Genesis 2, the problem addressed by two becoming one flesh is not childlessness but loneliness. In this biblical account, God mandates that two become one flesh not primarily to bear children but to display God's opposition to autonomy and isolation. In fact, Genesis 2—the creation account that explores most directly the relationship of male and female—says nothing about having children or being fruitful and multiplying.

In the context of current discussions in the church about the definition of marriage, we might also note that the partner that God created for the first human being is notable because of similarity, rather than difference. Unlike the animals that the first human creature had been naming, this creature who became a partner is said by the first one to at last be "bone of my bones and flesh of my flesh" (Gen. 2:23).

For centuries, the church has taught that the marriage partnership includes stereotyped gender roles embodied by men and women. It is striking that the second chapter of Genesis affirms the marriage partnership to be based on the humanity that the partners share in common rather than on their difference from or complementarity with each other, although the broader creation is surely a manifestation of God's delight in diversity.

Deuteronomy 23

As the sinful disintegration of human relationships through stereotyping and domination extends into the development of human tribes and nations, we see a conversation developing in the Bible about infertility and other marginalizing sexual experiences. Deuteronomy 23 offers a perspective that excludes all who do not conform to what is considered "normal" sexuality from the gathered worshiping community of God's people:

> No one whose testicles are crushed or whose penis is cut off shall be admitted to the assembly of the LORD. Those born of an illicit union shall not be admitted to the assembly of the LORD. Even to the tenth generation, none of their descendants shall be admitted to the assembly of the LORD. (Deut. 23:1-2; cf. also Lev. 21:17-21)

Here, sexual "normality" is treated as an identity marker and a boundary line for God's people. Men who cannot participate in "normal" sexual activity are excluded from the assembly of the Lord. The same is true of anyone whose birth is due to abnormal sexual activity, the result of an "illicit union."

The passage goes on to exclude those who are the result of mixed marriages in ethnic or national terms (e.g., mixed marriages between Israelites and Edomites or Moabites). Gerald Gerbrandt has pointed out that this exclusionary polity can be seen as the downside of a "close community of brothers and sisters" with a "strong identity" (405).

At the same time, the book of Ruth demonstrates that Obed, the grandfather of the beloved King David, was the result of such an illicit union between the Israelite Boaz and the Moabite Ruth. According to Deuteronomy 23, this fact alone should have disqualified at least seven of the kings of Israel and Judah: David, Solomon, Rehoboam, etc., from being part of the assembly of the Lord.

However, the story of Ruth seems designed to show that covenant faithfulness matters more than whether someone is an immigrant. Similarly, the author of Isaiah 56 argues that what really matters is justice and covenant loyalty, not how one is born. In naming the "immigrant" (v. 3) and the "eunuch" (v. 3), Isaiah appears to be engaging in intentional dialogue with Deuteronomy 23 (cf. also Wisdom of Solomon 3:14).

In contrast to the claims of the writer in Deuteronomy 23, Isaiah declares that God will give the sexually nonconforming eunuchs, who are unable to bear children but who keep the Sabbath, a "name better than sons and daughters...an everlasting name that shall not be cut off" (v. 5). In his commentary on Isaiah, Ivan Friesen concludes that the foundation for the inclusion of these outsiders is "their decision to belong to the Lord" and the resulting promise of "access to the spiritual life of Israel" which "replaces the prohibition in Deuteronomy 23:1" (352).

Leviticus 18:22, et al.

Bearing in mind the conversation in the Bible about what is "normal" or acceptable to God, let us consider several biblical passages that appear to contain words of condemnation for sexual intimacy between persons of the same sex. These passages include Leviticus 18:22; 20:13; Romans 1:26-27; 1 Corinthians 6:9; and 1 Timothy 1:10. As we consider what these passages of condemnation mean for us today, we would do well to consider whether human culture or God's perfect will is being displayed in these condemnations.

We often seriously underestimate the impact of culture in forming our sense of right and wrong. Leviticus itself bears witness to the fact that cultural sensibilities were relevant in 18:22 and 20:13. Both passages use the word *abomination* (or *toebah*) to describe same-gender intimacy. Other examples of *toebah* include Egyptians eating with Hebrews. That was an abomination to the Egyptians (Gen. 43:32). The Israelites' habit of raising sheep was also considered an abomination to the Egyptians (Gen. 46:34). Deuteronomy clearly says that cross-dressing is an abomination to God (22:5), and that putting money earned in prostitution into the offering is an abomination to God (23:18).

The texts about sexual intimacy from Leviticus are less clear about who considers the act abominable than are the texts about the Egyptians' scruples against eating with Hebrews or the passages opposing cross-dressing. In any event, the Bible does appear to recognize that the category of "abomination" is shaped by both human and divine attitudes.

Therefore, what people hold as "abominable" derives, at least in part, from cultural sensibilities. Although we generally like to imagine that God shares our particular cultural sensibilities, we know better. God's people must not simply follow the conventions of the worldly culture that surrounds them. Indeed, God's call, "Be holy, as I am holy" is in part a call to be separate, to be devoted, to not conform to the world (Rom. 12:1-2). It is a call to be Other, to be pilgrims and aliens in a foreign land (Heb. 11:13-14).

Nevertheless, all Christians today live out our discipleship in culturally specific ways. It is impossible to be "above" culture, since we live all of life within culture. We cannot simply avoid culture in expressing our faithfulness, yet we are called to distinguish our cultural sensibilities from the whispering voice of the Holy Spirit. Jesus, in his high priestly prayer, acknowledges this tension when he claims that his disciples "do not belong to the world" but that nevertheless, "I am not asking you to take them out of the world" (John 17:14-15).

Today we need to ask what it means to be "separated" in our sexual morality from the "abominable" practices of our surrounding culture, to "not belong to the world," while at the same time acknowledging that God speaks to us in the creation and the human cultures that derive from it.

Sometimes the church listens and adapts to surrounding cultural shifts to its own detriment, as exemplified by the church's frequent embrace of war and nationalism, leading to a church still divided by national and cultural identities and compromised by an idolatry of weapons. At other times, the church discovers its biblical voice in the social and cultural movements of human history.

For instance, 100 years ago, it was often considered "shameful" to be the result of sexual activity outside of marriage. Persons so born were called "illegitimate," or worse. However, cultural sensibilities on this issue have shifted. We now recognize that the circumstances of a person's conception do not add to or detract from that person's value or worth or that person's ability to love or be loved. Much of the church now recognizes that this cultural shift reflects the unconditional regard for the dignity of all human beings taught by Jesus Christ and displayed in his birth, life, death, and resurrection.

We also recognize that much of what is considered abominable or unclean in the legal literature of the Old Testament is reconsidered or redefined both within the prophetic literature of the Old Testament and within the moral universe of the New Testament. We will return to this New Testament redefinition of what is unclean in the next chapter.

Song of Songs

The Song of Songs is unique in Scripture and inconclusive when it comes to sexual ethics. Christina Bucher has suggested that this inconclusiveness perhaps "signifies that love cannot be quantified, packaged, and delivered up neatly" (Bailey and Bucher 251).

What is clear is that the Song is a celebration of love and of human sexuality, even if the author is less clear about what the limitations might be to that celebration. The lovers in the Song are not apparently married. They are clearly celebrating their awakening sexuality, and they delight in the beauty and pleasure of one another's bodies.

At the same time, they appear to feel hemmed in and limited by the more conservative expectations of others with regard to their sexual exploration, even if those limitations only add to their human desire: "many waters cannot quench love, neither can the floods drown it" (8:7). Phyllis Trible argues that this beautiful poetic depiction of unashamed human intimacy recalls the mutuality and harmony of the creation prior to the corruption of human relationships described in Genesis 2-3 as "the Song of Songs redeems a love story gone awry" (*Rhetoric* 144).

Throughout the centuries, the church has often avoided acknowledging the uninhibited celebration of erotic love in the Song of Songs by treating it as an allegory of the love that expresses the relationship between Christ and the church. Citing the display of love found in the Song of Songs, Menno writes that "so firm and ardent is love that it surpasses everything, conquers and con-

SEXUALITY IN THE BIBLE: OLD TESTAMENT • 61

sumes what is opposed to Christ and his Word, be it world
or flesh, tyrant or devil, sin or death, or whatever we may
think or name" (339). While the allegorical reading is a
valid way to interpret this text, it is also clear that the text
originally was written and affirmed by God's people as a
confirmation that erotic love is a gift and a blessing in itself, and not only as a prelude to childbearing or as a
metaphor for spiritual attachment: "love is strong as
death, passion fierce as the grave" (8:6).

STUDY QUESTIONS

1. What role does the difference between male and female bodies play in reflecting the image of God in human
beings?

2. Why is human companionship such a crucial component of a complete and "good" creation?

3. What are the aspects of companionship that define
marriage and distinguish it from other kinds of relationships? How might the permanence of marriage covenants
strengthen companionship? How might the patriarchal
habits associated with marriage—domination and role
rigidity, for example—undermine true companionship?

4. How has the church's sense of what is an "abomination" changed over time in response to cultural changes?
Give some examples of things that were once considered
"abominations" but are now understood to be acceptable.

5. How does the frank and poetic display of erotic desire in the Song of Songs compare with explicit and/or
pornographic representations of sexuality in popular culture today?

6. For what human qualities are you thankful as you
consider the human figure in the visual illustration at the
beginning of this chapter?

7. How are these human qualities enhanced by the ap-

pearance of a partner, as illustrated in the drawing at the beginning of chapter four (on the following page)? How does this illustration characterize the help offered by the partner?

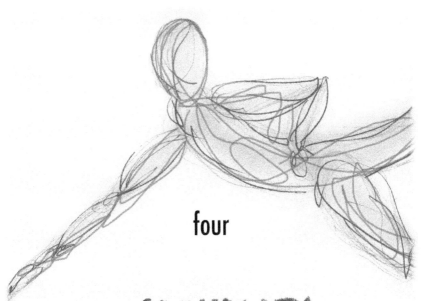

four

SEXUALITY IN THE BIBLE: NEW TESTAMENT

Chapter 4

SEXUALITY IN THE BIBLE: NEW TESTAMENT

As we turn to the new testament, we begin by recognizing that in the Gospels and in the teaching of the early church the concepts of what is unclean or an abomination are reconsidered. This change in perspective is nowhere illustrated more dramatically than in the vision received by the apostle Peter in Acts 10. To grasp the significance of this vision, it is helpful to review briefly the meaning of *abomination* in some Old Testament passages that are often cited in relationship to such matters as sexuality and food consumption.

Leviticus 18:22 and 20:13 both condemn a man having sex with another man because doing so is an "abomination" (*toebah* in Hebrew). That the very concept of abomination is in part a matter of cultural sensibilities was explored briefly in chapter 3. Also considered "abominable" in the Hebrew Bible is the eating of "unclean" foods. Deuteronomy 14:3 commands, for instance, "You shall not eat any abhorrent thing" (NRSV), such as ham or lobster.

A more literal translation from the Hebrew would read, "You shall not eat any abomination."

The word *abomination* or *abhorrent thing* (*toebah*) is the same word used in Leviticus 18:22 and 20:13. Ken Stone has pointed out that both food and sex function in the Mosaic law—and more generally in ancient religious cultures—as critical practices by which to differentiate a people from the surrounding nations.

> As eating and sexual intercourse involve the transgression of the body's boundaries, and the incorporation by the body of foreign substances, food and sex function as powerful symbolic markers of the boundaries between social units. (50)

Naming a specific food or sexual act an abomination is therefore a powerful way to establish identity in the ancient world—it is a way to know who we are as distinguished from and as unpolluted by other groups. However, as we will see, the early church found that following the way of Jesus Christ and listening to the Holy Spirit led toward dismantling these boundary markers in order to display God's reconciling love for all peoples.

ACTS 10

In Acts 10, God gives Peter the same vision three times while he is praying in a trance. Each time, a sheet comes down from heaven that is filled with unclean animals—*abominations*. Each time, God commands Peter to get up, kill, and eat. And each time, Peter refuses to do so, saying, "No way, Lord. I have never eaten an abomination!" In response, the voice from heaven says: "What God has made clean, you must not profane." Then the sheet is taken back up into heaven.

When the vision is over, Peter is puzzled about what it all meant. He is interrupted in his puzzled state by the presence of three men sent by Cornelius who are standing by Simon's gate.

Several important things are happening in this passage. First, God is saying to Peter that he must not "make common" or "make profane" what God has cleansed or made clean. The implication here is that these unclean foods that Peter has been avoiding are in fact *not* unclean. They are clean, not profane. Peter can and should eat them.

Second, the presence of several persons in the flesh at Simon's gate forces Peter to translate the insight of his dream into action.

What is going on here? We see another dialogue within the Bible about cleanness and uncleanness. It is clear in context that this vision or dream was meant to show Peter that he should not avoid Gentiles but should, in fact, accept and bless them.

This may have been at first too abstract and theoretical for Peter to handle. But the presence of real-life human beings waiting at the gate did not allow Peter the luxury of leaving the matter in the abstract. He needed time—but not unlimited time!—to learn that God is not partial to some compared to others. These three men needed some kind of response—a response from Peter. Likewise, the "issue of homosexuality" is not an abstract topic facing the church today; real-life human beings are standing at the gate.

Jesus repeatedly crossed the boundaries of purity to be in relationship with people. God's words to Peter in his vision, "What God has made clean, you must not profane" (Acts 10:15; cf. 11:9), must be taken seriously because they reflect Jesus' priority of relationships over purity. Might well-meaning Christians risk profaning what God has made clean when they oppose commitments of love and marriage that gays and lesbians wish to make? In so doing, might they risk standing with "purity" against Jesus and against love? We suggest that the church today can instead thank God for the reality of loving relationships and for the desire to bear public witness to that love in a covenant ceremony.

Acts 10 suggests that traditional conceptions of what is abominable can and should be reconsidered by anyone who seeks to respond to the real needs of flesh-and-blood human beings today, just as Peter did. As we will see below, Jesus urges such reconsideration in the way that he interprets the Scriptures. Likewise, Peter's experience with the vision of a sheet and the visit of Cornelius illustrates what such reconsideration of abominations of food and sex might mean in the life of the church.

LUKE 7:36-50

Jesus was criticized for inadequately separating the clean from the unclean in his own ministry. When the woman of Luke 7 wept and bathed Jesus' feet with her tears and dried them with her hair, Simon the Pharisee was secretly critical of Jesus' lack of moral perception. In response, Jesus says, "Simon, do you see this woman?" Jesus draws attention to the presence of a real human being and his words make clear that he values love (v. 47), forgiveness (vv. 47-48), and faith (v. 50) more than artificial boundaries between people.

Luke 7 suggests that we should maintain a proper biblical perspective on priorities. For us a biblical perspective means following Jesus in valuing love, forgiveness, and faith above boundaries between people. Such boundaries often feel natural but are in fact culturally constructed and therefore open to godly challenge and Christ-like transgression. Might Jesus be asking us today as we debate the inclusion of persons who do not conform with traditional expressions of sexuality in the church: "Do you see this woman? Do you see this man?" To be sure, when we genuinely see the other as Jesus did we are likely to discover as Simon did that crossing boundaries may often be an outcome of forgiveness, rather than a cause for it.

Matthew 19:10-12

At the conclusion of Jesus' challenging teaching that divorce, except for "unchastity," is forbidden, Jesus' disciples respond with amazement: "If such is the case of a man with his wife, it is better not to marry." But he said to them,

> "Not everyone can accept this teaching, but only those to whom it is given. For there are eunuchs who have been so from birth, and there are eunuchs who have been made eunuchs by others, and there are eunuchs who have made themselves eunuchs for the sake of the kingdom of heaven. Let anyone accept this who can." (vv. 11-12)

As challenging as Jesus' statement about divorce and remarriage is in today's context, Jesus' statement about eunuchs is mysterious. Its exact relationship with Jesus' teaching about divorce is not immediately apparent. It appears that Jesus is making a statement about people whose sexuality does not conform to the social expectations of heterosexual marriage. Jesus begins and ends with the statement acknowledging that not everyone can accept this teaching.

Jesus gives three categories of eunuchs here: those who have been eunuchs from birth, those who were made eunuchs by others, and those who made themselves eunuchs. The first category encompasses people for whom heterosexual marriage is not an option. The second category likely refers to men who were castrated and were therefore unable to engage in a conventional heterosexual relationship. The third category likely refers to self-imposed celibacy for the sake of the reign of God. All of these ways of being a eunuch signify as "unmanly" in the ancient world of the Bible (Wilson 119-125).

What unites Jesus' saying about eunuchs with his teaching about divorce and also with the disciples' amazement is the suggestion that sexual obligation toward another is or should be more than a matter of convenience or satisfaction of desire—it is instead a matter that involves promises and constraints, including possibly a promise of celibacy. This view of sexuality challenges both ancient masculinity and the culture of gratification associated with modern consumerism.

Marriage should not be a patriarchal marketplace controlled by masculine privilege or whim. Marriage partners should not divorce simply because they grow tired of each other and wish for a new partner or wish to make a lifestyle change; sex implies and entails long-term obligation and commitment.

That is why sexual intimacy, with its implied obligations of care and devotion between companions, can compromise an unqualified commitment to Christian discipleship and the coming reign of God. Celibacy frees disciples for complete devotion to Jesus Christ and to one another. At the same time, Jesus' insistence that not everyone can accept this teaching implies that it is not necessarily a rule for all of his disciples. Some latitude for individual calling and perspective must be factored into decisions about intimate relationships and celibacy. Some of God's children will do well to maintain celibacy in devotion to God's reign, but such celibacy must not be imposed on them. Some can accept it; some cannot.

Matthew 19 suggests that sexual fulfillment remains at some level a matter of personal discernment and calling. But marriage and traditional family life clearly do not have a privileged status in the coming reign of God or among Jesus' disciples. Neither should it be so in the church.

ACTS 15

Acts 15 records what was probably the most difficult and divisive issue in the early church: Must newly converted Gentile men be circumcised? Although Luke shows an interest in downplaying disagreements in the church, he does not downplay this one, since he characterizes the disagreements as intense and the dialogue as sharp. The contemporary church can learn from Acts 15 that conflict is normal in church life, and it can also find clues about how to discern well amidst disagreement.

It seems likely that if this issue were confronting the church today, we would call conferences to study Genesis 17, the key Scripture demanding circumcision. In that passage God makes clear that if they wish to participate in God's covenant Abraham and all of his male descendants must be circumcised; that is, each one must have the foreskin surgically removed from his penis. It was not optional. It is therefore reasonable to ask, "What did the early church not understand about Genesis 17? Was Genesis 17 not clear to them? Didn't they *know* about this text?"

The church definitely knew about this text, and it seems probable that someone at the meeting in Jerusalem appealed to it, even though Luke does not report this in Acts 15. It is clear that *other* Scriptures factored into the argument. For instance, in Acts 15:16-18, James quotes from Amos 9:11-12 in the Septuagint—the Greek translation of the Hebrew Bible that was in common use when the New Testament was written. The Greek Septuagint version of Amos 9:11-12 differs from the Hebrew text of this same passage—stressing the future inclusion of all the Gentiles in the restoration of Israel. James also alludes to Isaiah 45:21 which emphasizes that this inclusive vision was from "of old."

These passages support the idea that the inclusion of the Gentiles is not some shocking new departure from tradition, but was part of God's plan all along. The circumcision-requiring faction in the meeting at Jerusalem just needed to look at things in a new way.

Scripture was not the only resource upon which these believers drew at the Jerusalem meeting. They also told stories about how the Holy Spirit was changing the lives of some of these Gentiles. Both those who wanted to require circumcision and those who did not appealed to tradition. And they argued about it, using their reason and understanding to explore the issue and to persuade others. In the end, the five elements of reason, experience, Scripture, tradition, and the voice of the Holy Spirit all played a role in the church's rethinking of this issue.

Acts 15 suggests that in discerning whether God blesses same-sex marriage, the church would do well to employ the same means of understanding that the early church employed in discerning the matter of circumcision: reason, experience, Scripture, tradition, and the voice of the Holy Spirit. At least that would be the *scriptural* way to approach it.

1 Corinthians 7

In 1 Corinthians 7, Paul presents heterosexual marriage as a compromise in kingdom values—not an unfaithful compromise that should be avoided at all costs, but an acceptable compromise. What is best is to remain single, celibate, in service to God's reign.

At the same time, "it is better to marry than to burn" (v. 9). In *The Christian Century*, theologian Gerald Schlabach offers an eloquent explanation about how we might understand what it means "to burn" or "to marry" in this passage:

> "To burn" may stand for all the ways that we human beings, left to ourselves, live only for ourselves, our own pleasures, and our own survival. By contrast, "to marry" may signal the way that all of us (even those who do so in a vocation of lifelong celibacy) learn to bend our desires away from ourselves, become vulnerable to the desires of others, and bend toward the service of others. That is a good thing for all. (23)

The metaphor of fire for sexual desire was common in Hellenistic literature. Paul, like many (though not all) of his Hellenistic Jewish counterparts, seems to have thought of sexual desire not according to categories of right and wrong (as if there were legitimate and illegitimate kinds of sexual desire), but rather on a scale of, we might say, quantity.

For some people, sexual desire builds over time, leading to a kind of "burning." For such people it was better to rid oneself of the tension associated with desire through sexual intercourse in marriage than it was to continue in the state of growing and (ultimately) uncontrollable desire.

Thus in Paul's writings sex in marriage is not so much the expression of appropriate sexual desire as it is the one sanctioned way to extinguish desire. This view is quite different from most views of heterosexual married sex in contemporary Christianity.

Paul's view of desire as an excess that can be rightly extinguished or managed within an intimate covenant relationship is relevant to our interpretation of the passages in Romans 1 that appear to condemn same-sex intimacy (24-27). The problem with some same-sex relationships that Paul identifies is that they serve the creature rather than the creator and reflect idolatry rather than the worship of God (Toews 71).

James Brownson has explained that the self-centered and idolatrous relationships that Paul names in Romans 1:24-27 are not descriptions of people who are expressing naturally given "homosexual" desires but rather who are "driven to ever more exotic and unnatural forms of stimulation in the pursuit of pleasure" (156). The problem with the relationships opposed by Paul, in other words, is that they express excessive desire beyond what is natural.

More broadly, Paul's evaluation of homoerotic human intimacy seems to be based on his assumption that it was focused exclusively inward rather than being open to the obligations of child bearing, service to others, relational love, or a hospitable household. Certainly we see examples of such a view of homoerotic relationships in Hellenistic philosophy that was influencing educated Jewish leaders like Paul.

Writers and teachers like Plato had preferred homoerotic relationships among male students and teachers (relationships best described as pederasty) to the procreative sex associated with heterosexual relationships and households involving women and children who were considered distractions. Intimacy between male teachers and students was understood to serve the development of shared ideas and knowledge; in contrast, heterosexual intimacy led to children and household obligations. In his extensive discussion of Greek homoerotic pederasty, Martti Nissinen summarizes Plato's appreciation for "the pederastic relationship as the noblest of all human relations and as the embodiment of the purest love" (59).

Like Plato, Paul understands procreative heterosexual relationships to be a distraction from the higher calling of serving and understanding the divine will. Unlike Plato,

Paul entertains the possibility that the covenant obligations connected with procreative intimacy in marriage can support the life of love and service to which Christians are called in the church.

In our own cultural setting, intimate same-sex relationships are commonly expressed within the context of covenant obligations that we associate with marriage, a possibility that does not seem to have occurred to Paul. Might we be able to understand Paul's dictum that "it is better to marry than to burn" to apply to same-sex covenants as well?

Some Christians, including Mennonite scholars like Willard Swartley, interpret the vice lists in 1 Corinthians 6:9 and I Timothy 1:10 to mean that all same-sex intimacy is excluded from the kingdom of God (68-71). Other Mennonite scholars, among the more prominent being C. Norman Kraus, challenge this interpretation (*On Being Human* 76-77).

The combination of the Greek terms *malakoi* and *arsenokoitai* are sometimes translated to mean "homosexual." Such solid evangelical Christian scholars as James Brownson and ethicist David Gushee suggest the reference is likely instead to specific sexual roles (i.e. passive younger boys and active older men) and not to sexual orientation per se (Brownson 274).

In any event, such practices as pederasty, male prostitution, and coercive exploitation within which same-sex relations were sometimes expressed in the pagan culture that surrounded the early church are clearly condemned in these passages. But the compiler of these vice lists seems unlikely to have had in mind a loving exclusive relationship of intimacy as part of the same list that includes liars, adulterers, thieves, and slave traders.

Following his thorough examination of the terms *malakoi* and *arsenokoitai*, Dale Martin urges us to acknowledge that while we probably will be unable to confirm without question what Paul intended to mean with these terms, we are nevertheless obligated to interpret these texts according to the rule of love: "any interpretation of Scripture that hurts people, oppresses people, or destroys people cannot be the right interpretation, no matter how traditional, historical, or exegetically respectable" (50). In other words, we should read the Bible with the same kind of unqualified love for God and neighbor that Jesus exemplified in his reading and interpretation of Scripture.

Some remarkable points connect the teachings of Jesus and Paul in Matthew 19 and 1 Corinthians 7. Both Jesus and Paul seem to suggest that celibacy is the best course. However, both also suggest that this high calling may not be appropriate for all people. For those people, sex must not be divorced from love and commitment—the hard and holy work of marriage. As Gerald Schlabach puts it, marriage is "the communally sealed bond of lifelong intimate mutual care between two people that creates humanity's most basic unit of kinship, thus allowing human beings to build sustained networks of society" (24).

Paul insists in this passage that the expression of sexual desire finds its proper home in an exclusive relationship of love and commitment rather than in the marketplace of human autonomy. If so, Christians should encourage marriage for church members in same-sex relationships rather than just allow it. At the same time, perhaps Christians need to renew our appreciation for marriage more broadly as an expression of Christian discipleship—bending toward the service of others—rather than as a moral or social status marker for heterosexual couples.

Just as importantly, Paul's counsel on marriage and singleness in 1 Corinthians 7 displays humility with regard to his authority. In v. 10 he issues a command that he says is not a matter of personal opinion, but comes from the Lord. But most of what he says in 1 Corinthians 7 he presents as his own opinion, not a command from the Lord, even if Paul commends his opinion as worthwhile and worth taking seriously (see esp. vv. 10, 25b, 40).

1 Corinthians 7 connects with Matthew 19 in suggesting that because love and marriage are profoundly personal issues, these are things that should not be forced on others, and people are wise to recognize that sexual fulfillment isn't everything. In fact, men and women are blessed if they feel prepared to commit to God's reign in a state of celibacy without giving physical expression to their sexual desires. However, the expression of sexual desire within a committed relationship does have a place for Christians and those who elect to express those desires physically are not wrong in doing so, *as long as they are expressed in the context of love and commitment between two persons—that is, within a marriage covenant.*

In any event, the New Testament authors are unanimous in speaking with one voice in condemning "sexual immorality"—*porneia* in the Greek. This voice does not, however, define clearly what porneia is.

For instance, does it remain incumbent upon brothers-in-law to impregnate childless sisters-in-law whose husbands have died (cf. Deut. 25:5-10; Ruth 4)? Is it okay for a man to have more than one wife, as long as he is not an overseer or a deacon (1 Tim. 3:2, 12)? Most careful treatments of this issue conclude that the context in 1 Timothy indicates that what is at stake is the reputation of the leader in the community. As Paul Zehr puts it in his commentary on 1 Timothy, "infidelity to the covenant commitment to one's spouse in marriage often destroys the fabric of trust that is essential for effective and credible church leadership" (79).

Thus, what is required is that a leader be a "one-woman man" (1 Tim. 3:2, 12) or a "one-man woman" (1

Tim. 5:9). Rather than a proscription against (1) polygamy, or (2) divorce and remarriage, or (3) remarriage after the death of a spouse, these passages call for faithfulness toward one's spouse. In other words, they call for leaders to avoid porneia.

But again, what is porneia, other than infidelity toward one's spouse? Thomas Yoder-Neufeld has pointed to the association of porneia or sexual immorality with greed in scriptures such as Ephesians 5:3. Seen this way, sexual immorality can be defined as wanting and taking more than what properly belongs to us, without regard for personal integrity and covenantal obligations, thus leading to abuse, adultery, and the "defilement of the holiness of God's people" (Yoder-Neufeld 228).

Finally, it is important to remember the context for Paul's extensive discussion of marriage in 1 Corinthians 7 as a valid alternative to a preferred single blessedness. The context is the confession in the previous chapter that our bodies are "members of Christ" (1 Cor. 6:15). For Paul, and for Anabaptist Christians, this relationship with Jesus Christ through membership in his body by baptism is the most profound and truthful expression of the "help" that we need to be most fully human. The body and community of Christ endures while the "present form of this world is passing away" and this embracing Christly body is thus the ultimate home for our vulnerable and lonely human bodies (1 Cor. 7:31).

STUDY QUESTIONS

1. What are examples of behaviors once considered "unclean" or "abominable" but now deemed "clean?" What behaviors once thought "clean" are now "unclean?"

2. In what ways does marriage undermine or support the mission of the church?

3. How should the church value singleness and celibacy in relationship to marriage and sexual intimacy? In what ways does the church reflect or compromise the New Testament vision of traditional family life to have lower priority in the church than brotherly and sisterly relationships in the body of Christ?

4. Can same-sex covenantal unions serve the same purpose that Paul ascribes to heterosexual marriage? Why or why not?

5. How does marriage interact with sexual desire: Does it provide a safe space for uninhibited expression of desire? Or does it extinguish the tension of desire?

6. What kind of desire and attachment is expressed in the human relationship illustrated in the drawing at the beginning of this chapter?

7. How is the image of human relationship developed in the picture of communal attachment as displayed in the drawing at the beginning of chapter five (on the following page)?

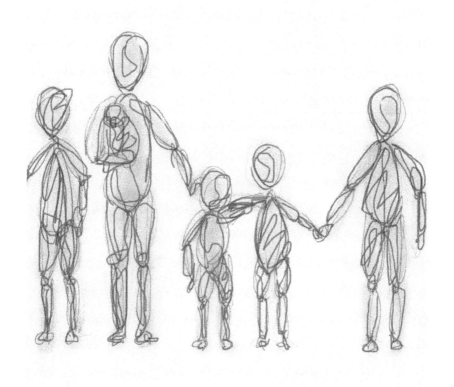

five

MORAL
CHALLENGES
FOR THE
CHURCH

Chapter 5

MORAL CHALLENGES FOR THE CHURCH

IN THIS CHAPTER WE POSE SOME QUESTIONS about our moral obligations to one another given the changing and often conflicted understandings of sexual identity and morality. We believe the church is obliged to attend to the political context in which these questions of sex and gender identity are being addressed.

In the cultural setting of North America, it is becoming increasingly clear that people have been created by God to experience sexuality in a diversity of ways. On the one hand, a majority of people identify with the gender they are assigned at birth and experience sexual attraction in a predominantly heterosexual way (attraction between male and female).

On the other hand, there are also lesbian women who are primarily attracted to women; gay men who are attracted to men; bisexual men and women who are attracted to both men and women; transgender men and women whose biological sex did not or does not match their gender identity (e.g. a person assigned biological maleness at birth who identifies as a woman); questioning or queer people who do not conform to conventional sex or gender identities; intersex people whose bodily sex characteristics do not fit the definitions of a male or female body; asexual people who experience little or no sexual attraction to other people; and more.

The acronym that is currently used to include all of these sexually "nonconforming" people is LGBTQIA+ (lesbian, gay, bisexual, transgendered, queer/questioning, intersex, asexual, and more). The + acknowledges that even this list of categories does not fully encompass all the ways in which people experience sexuality and gender differently from people who are primarily heterosexual or whose gender experience aligns with their assigned sex (cisgender).

The theology of Scripture outlined in previous chapters and our approach (in light of it) to a variety of biblical texts in both the Old Testament and New Testament demonstrate a way of being biblical in moral discernment that paves the way for the full inclusion of persons who identify as lesbian, gay, bisexual, transgender, intersex, questioning, or asexual (LGBTQIA+) in Christian congregations, including the blessing of same-sex marriages.

For the renewed and embracing church that God is bringing about, welcome is the watchword. Like the formerly forbidden eunuchs and immigrants who are welcomed to the assembly of the LORD in Isaiah 56, LGBTQIA+ believers are now full participants in the spiritual life of this church that is on the way. We understand this welcome to include receiving with gratitude the spiritual gifts of all our brothers and sisters, including the credentialing (licensing and ordaining) of LGBTQIA+ persons on the same basis as heterosexual individuals, whether single or in a covenanted relationship.

There remain, however, many implications of this emerging inclusive path for congregations and other church networks to discuss. The inclusive posture suggested here continues to be tested as congregations embrace, rather than simply tolerate, membership for LGBTQIA+ people, as pastors begin to offer same-sex covenant and marriage ceremonies to parishioners, and as the conference credentials sexually nonconforming people for ministry.

At the same time, some congregations continue to discern and discuss, some arriving at different conclusions than the inclusive practices toward which this study guide point. Some church members are understandably reluctant to accept practices that the church has traditionally opposed in its confessions and membership rules. Others are convinced that the vice lists from 1 Corinthians 6 and 1 Timothy 1 discussed in the previous chapter include prohibitions of same-sex intimacy in any setting. Many people who hold differing views about same-sex covenants share a desire for the church to provide moral guidance about sexual intimacy in a corrupting context shaped by individualism and consumer culture—a context that poses moral challenges to all of us, whatever our sexual orientation.

In this chapter we consider the moral challenges faced by the church in its discernment and policy decisions related to sexual and gender identity. In the following chapter we suggest ways for the church to provide moral guidance to persons making choices about sexual intimacy and marriage.

SEXUALITY AND CHARACTER

As we address sexuality and character, we should first acknowledge that Mennonites in North America live in a culture that privileges certain (white, Protestant, male-centered) versions of heterosexuality. By this we mean that in literature, media culture, advertising, and political leadership we see the dominant depiction of a "normal" family as based in a romantic heterosexual relationship between a white man and a white woman that leads to marriage and children, often based on patriarchal assumptions arising from a conventional interpretation of Genesis 2 to accept rather than critique role differentiation and male privilege.

In Anglo-American cultures, this privileged vision of family life is bolstered by a standard marriage plot such as is displayed, for example, in classic romance novels like Jane Austen's *Pride and Prejudice* and reiterated endlessly in Hollywood romantic comedies from *It's a Wonderful Life* to *My Big Fat Greek Wedding*. This standard plot involves the experience of romantic attraction or "falling in love" that is posed against the expectations or impediments of family, community, and culture. In the many variations of this story "true love" triumphs over numerous social, financial, political, and psychological obstacles and establishes a family unit that is a self-actualizing haven from the surrounding world.

This hugely popular plot provides a framework for "normal" intimacy against which all relationships tend to be measured and found wanting. Other forms of intimate relationship exhibited in our culture then appear as exceptions to the rule of what is sometimes called white "heteronormativity"—the patterns of sexual intimacy associated with a specific idealized vision of white heterosexual couples and their families.

There are a number of moral problems with this white heteronormativity. First, we fail to notice the diversity of sexual relationships testified to in the biblical tradition, as well as the curse of male domination found in Genesis 2.

Second, we ignore how both the Gospels and Pauline literature relativize the forms that intimate relationships take. The Gospels and the writings identified with Paul focus instead on the *character* of those relationships. In the Bible, the character of a relationship involves such matters as whether the partners act in loving ways with one another, care for each other, yield to one another's needs and desires, and express the love and fidelity of Jesus Christ in their union (Eph. 5:21-23).

One of the great gifts offered to the church by the LGBTQIA+ movement is that we have been challenged to develop a deeper and more truthful account of faithful intimacy than that provided by the *Confession of Faith in a Mennonite Perspective*, Article 19, which defines "right sexual union" as intimacy between a man and a woman who are married. Surely the form of heterosexual marriage is not a sufficient criterion for good sex since it does not account for the many ways in which sexual intercourse can be profoundly immoral even when practiced within marriage.

In the context of contemporary debates about sexual relationships in the Christian tradition we find that the form of a relationship cannot be simply identified with its character. The form of a relationship—whether two men, two women, a man and a woman, before or after a marriage license—tells us little about the content, attitudes, and moral behavior between the persons involved in the relationship.

If we commit to following the teachings of Jesus and Paul, let us not too easily identify moral qualities with a specific form. Instead, let us ask what practices of intimacy reflect the loving and serving way of Jesus Christ, rather than the selfish and privilege-maintaining ways of the world.

SEXUALITY AND VIOLENCE

The church must also face the moral challenge represented by the relationship between sexuality and violence. The practice of "othering"—marginalizing people because of the identities they bear—is the first step toward violence. Violence begins with dehumanizing: rejecting or ignoring that which is human, made in the image of God, and reducing another person to the social roles or identities they display. Such violence can include regarding a person primarily as a sexual object or in terms of a gender role, thus justifying behaviors that demean and abuse. The extensive availability and popularity of degrading pornography through the Internet is a troubling example of such dehumanizing and abusive attitudes and practices.

Violence also involves differences in and misuses of power. Othering and marginalization in European-originated cultures depends upon a hierarchy of identities that places whiteness, maleness, and heterosexuality at the top, while subordinating other identities. As noted above, straight, white males are often considered to be the "norm" whether this assumption is consciously promoted or subconsciously held. In Drew Hart's recent book on racism and the church, he describes this "myth of the superior white male figure" as an idolatry that contrasts with the "crucified and risen Lord" that Christians are called instead to emulate (160). As Hart puts it, "the church must become the people who renounce lording over others in all manners, whether white supremacy, patriarchy, or economic domination" (160).

We are only now beginning to come to terms with the license to abuse women and children that many men have exercised from their positions of authority in the church, in schools, in family life, and in other social institutions. As Carolyn Holderread Hegen and others have documented eloquently, this combination of unquestioned power and sexual objectification has left a dangerous and hurtful legacy of great violence that blasphemes the image of God represented in human beings.

Human identity is more complex than the boxes checked off for race, gender, and so on. As children of God we are more than a sum of individual social identities and we are called to no longer regard each other from a merely human point of view (2 Cor. 5:16). We are called instead as members of the body of Christ to give special honor to the "less respectable" members of this body—that is, to those with low status according to conventional wisdom (2 Cor. 12:23-25).

This is how the church is called to challenge the "human point of view" that leads to exclusion and violence. In order to do this, we need to understand more fully how this "human point of view" is built around exclusion of the Other at many levels.

Although a particular dimension of identity, or way of being, may stand out more for some individuals than others, it is critical to realize that various forms of oppression and exclusion are based on the very structures of meaning and identity that we rely on to know who we are. Whether we are "white" or "gay" or "female" determines the ways we have learned to relate to one another in society— whether from a position of advantage and control or from a position of disadvantage and deference (or even guilt). In such a context, all the ways in which a person does not fit a white, masculine, and heterosexual (and therefore triply privileged) identity begin to pile up and amplify alienation from communities that are organized around such markers as whiteness, masculinity, and heterosexual attraction.

Closely related to these privileges is a certain ideal of family life—often expressed as "family values" in American culture—that assumes the normalcy and desirability of a "nuclear" family headed by a father and nurtured by a mother who gives birth to two or three children. This model is often assumed to be "biblical" even though it does not fit the tribal vision of family life that is more typical in the Bible. Yet those who do not belong to such a two-parent nuclear family are often regarded in our society as incomplete or flawed. The church all too frequently reflects rather than challenges this prejudice against those who fall short of "family values."

The point here is that marginalization and oppression do not act independently of one another but instead are related together, creating structures, habits, and attitudes that can be collectively experienced as profoundly violent. How do our congregations unknowingly continue to marginalize and exclude at multiple levels? How have they done so not just by playing different marginalized groups off one another (asserting that to support one marginal identity requires opposing another, for example), but in other ways as well? How have our congregations said to people, "Your very existence is a threat to the order of our community and thus is unacceptable?"

By contrast, how might our congregations learn to appreciate all of the ways in which we are created differently and all of the ways we love differently as gifts to the body of Christ that derive from the same spirit? How might we begin to reject in our church polities the idea that everyone needs to express love and desire in the same way? How might we give special honor to those who are regarded by our society as the least respectable (1 Cor. 12:22-26)? How might we display God's blessing of the poor and the persecuted in our churches (Matt. 5:1-11)?

SEXUALITY AND CULTURE

Jesus' own love for those on the margins—the tax collectors, the prostitutes, and others from the "wrong side of the tracks"—was scandalous in his day. More specifically, Jesus displayed a countercultural welcome of those who were not regarded as acceptable company because of the form of their intimate relationships, such as the Samaritan woman at the well who was not married to the man with whom she was living (John 4:18).

By contrast, most Christians simply find "reasonable" and "acceptable" those sexual expressions that somehow make sense in their cultural context. As we respond to Jesus' welcome of persons whose lives do not correspond with dominant cultural norms—including norms that persist within the church—we realize that the church is called to display God's welcome across a large variety of different cultures. How do we practice welcome and discern sexual ethics in a global church that includes dramatically different cultural settings and assumptions?

Does the North American church have anything to say to Kenyan Christians about polygamy? Does the Kenyan church have anything to say to the North American church about fidelity and honor in marriage? How could congregations go about demonstrating that they possess the intercultural competence and historical consciousness necessary to address sexual ethics across many cultures fairly and honestly, including the possibility that there may be space for a diversity of practices across the church, just as there is in the Bible? Most importantly, how can the church learn to display in a variety of cultural contexts the loving welcome of people whose lives do not conform to varying cultural expectations, sexual and otherwise?

Throughout human history it has been common for one man to partner with one woman in conjugal relations, even though there have also been other forms of intimate partnership, as we have seen in the Bible. Sexual intimacy between one man and one woman—and the marriage and family life that often flourish as a context for such intimacy—are likely to continue as a conventional practice, even though there have always been other ways in which human beings express sexual desire and experience intimacy.

The question is this: How should people of faith think about those of us not represented in that conventional majority experience? Is majority sexual expression automatically good and minority sexual expression automatically suspect? Or is all sexual expression potentially good in the context of covenant practices of love and fidelity?

Mennonite pastor Meghan Good writes that, "sex is a mirror" that either "reflects the true God or it reflects idolatry." Perhaps this question of whether our practices of sexuality reflect godly love or human idolatry is a better way to frame the moral challenge for the church than whether the church is embracing or enforcing the dominant form of sexuality in our culture.

STUDY QUESTIONS

1. How much attention should the church give to the *form* of a sexual relationship (the types and roles of the persons involved) in determining its moral qualities? Does our congregational culture reinforce or challenge the "marriage plot" of white heterosexual romance?

2. In what ways might an intimate relationship exhibit a corrupted or harmful character even though it takes place within a marriage?

3. How can the church challenge abusive and violent patterns of behavior in marriages, in institutions, and in society? How should the church respond, for example, to the consumption of pornography?

4. What might it mean for the church to give special honor to those of its members who do not conform to conventional relationship practices—those that are regarded in our culture as "less honorable" from a merely human point of view (see 1 Cor. 12:22-26)?

5. How should churches and conferences who are committed to full membership, marriage, and ministry leadership for LGBTQIA+ persons respond to churches and conferences who interpret the Bible to oppose such inclusion and who are offended by such decisions?

6. How is welcome and belonging displayed in the visual illustration at the beginning of this chapter?

7. What experiences of inclusion or exclusion are brought to mind by studying the visual illustration at the beginning of this chapter?

six

MORAL
CHOICES
FOR
BELIEVERS

Chapter 6

MORAL CHOICES FOR BELIEVERS

IN THIS FINAL CHAPTER we consider several moral features of sexual intimacy. These features focus more on how people treat one another (character) than on the social identities of the partners in a relationship (form).

LISTENING TO THE CHURCH

The first moral choice is whether we will listen to the voice of the church in our decisions about sexual intimacy. Even though the church has misread the Bible in ways that harm and hurt (e.g. through abuse, exclusion, etc.), the Bible has also served as a resource for challenging those hurtful actions and decisions.

A decision to give the church a voice in our moral choices about sexual intimacy is not a choice simply to submit to the church's authority over us. Rather, it is a choice to be a part of the church, to give and receive counsel, to wrestle together with what the Bible is saying to us, and to bring our personal choices into conversation with Scripture and the collective discernment of the church.

This kind of attention to the voice of the church displays how sexually intimate relationships can flourish when they are opened to what David Matzko McCarthy calls a "wider order of love." As two people become attached to one another through the experience of sexual intimacy and life partnership, their relationship is most fully expressed within a larger network of relationships, including, for example, extended family, friendship circles, and church relationships.

Furthermore, a thriving sexual union nourishes not only its own household but also the larger network of which it is a part and, in fact, helps shape that network through its character. Involving the church in the formation of sexually intimate relationships can help to strengthen truly hospitable and sustainable unions—relationships of intimacy that are turned generously outward toward the world rather than focused exclusively inward toward one another.

A beautiful love story that illustrates such accountability to a faith community and generosity to others is found in the book of Tobit, which is part of Catholic Bibles but considered apocryphal by most Protestants. For several centuries Anabaptist communities regarded "apocryphal" books like Tobit as scripture, and most Amish weddings today still recount the risky romance of Tobias and Sarah from the book of Tobit.

Tobias and Sarah are the only children in each of their families and so their families' prospects for the future rest on decisions about love that they will make. Tobias' family faces economic challenges and Sarah's family is traumatized by a demon that terrorizes Sarah.

When Tobias undertakes a journey away from his parents' city to a far country in order to recover money belonging to the family, he is accompanied by the angel Raphael. Rapahel is disguised as a human companion who instructs Tobias on how to conduct himself when he seeks to be married to his cousin, Sarah—an obligation since she is a widow and Tobias is the closest living male relative (Deut. 25:5-10).

It turns out that Sarah has been married seven times with each husband dying during the wedding night before the marriage is consummated. The husbands are killed by a demon that stalks Sarah and is jealous of her husbands.

When Tobias finds out about Sarah's worrisome past, he understandably has second thoughts. But Raphael reminds him of his father's instructions to marry one of his own people and reassures him that if he takes precautions on his wedding night, the sex will be safe. These precautions include praying to God for mercy and protection while roasting the heart and liver from a fish on hot coals prior to intercourse so that the odor chases away the demon.

When Tobias hears these words of Raphael, he begins to love Sarah, even though he has not yet seen her. When he and Sarah meet they address one another as brother and sister in God's family and are encouraged in their choice to risk marriage by Sarah's parents.

By contrast with the marriage plot referenced in chapter 5, the risky romance of Tobias and Sarah is intertwined with the faithful romance of God's covenant people. Being part of God's people and God's story strengthens rather than undermines the love of Tobias and Sarah and provides a supportive and flourishing context for sexual intimacy. On their wedding night prior to intercourse they follow the angel's instructions—praying to God for safety and roasting the fish liver—with the outcome that the demon flees to Egypt and the couple is safe.

The marriage of Tobias and Sarah is shown in the book of Tobit to contribute to the health and well being of their extended families and neighbors. Tobias' father Tobit is healed of his blindness, their family's financial stability is restored, the bonds between two families are strengthened, and much joy and celebration accompany the couple's nuptials.

When Raphael offers some marriage counseling to the happy couple he does not tell them to have children but instead encourages them to be generous: "It is better to give alms than to lay up gold" (Tob. 12:8-9). This story illustrates well how true love is larger than romantic attraction and safe sex requires more than birth control. Good sex is accountable to the wisdom of the community and is attentive to the past experiences or traumas of each partner. And, as the story illustrates, good sex is accompanied by joy and generosity—leading sometimes to children but even more importantly to gifts for the poor.

KEEPING COVENANT

A second moral choice involves our covenant obligations. These include the obligations to our covenant with God through baptism, to the covenant with our partner through marriage and covenant union, and to the covenant with our church family through membership and communion. The most important of all of these is our baptismal vow.

Do our actions expressing love and intimacy with another person contribute to the resurrection life into which we have been raised in baptism? For example, are our expressions of love and intimacy consistent with the reconciling and peacemaking life of a disciple of Jesus? Is this expression of intimacy honest in what it says about our intentions and commitments?

In an article in *The Christian Century*, Katherine Willis Pershey calls attention to how fidelity within the marriage covenant bears witness to the fidelity of God in the biblical covenant. According to Pershey, "infidelity in marriage is intimately related to infidelity to God—because each is a covenant relationship"(21). By contrast, "the consequence of mutual fidelity is a life steeped in blessings" (23). For Pershey, this commitment to covenant fidelity can be "very sexy" because of the freedom for adventurous and vulnerable intimacy that is provided within the boundaries of covenant (20-21).

Thus we should consider whether we are able to offer the care and fidelity of covenant that is suggested by sexual intimacy. Are we open to the joint mission and calling implied by the union of two people and bodies? Are we prepared to parent and support children that are born as a result of this union or that may be cared for or adopted by the household that arises from the union?

In the biblical tradition, the marriage relationship is a covenant that makes clear the commitments that protect intimate sexual relationships from betrayal and exploitation. The moral character of an intimate relationship is determined partly by whether the sexual intimacy is in keeping with the terms of the marriage covenant. A question to consider then is whether sexual intimacy in a specific relationship betrays or supports the spirit of the marriage covenant, which requires two people to be exclusive as well as to feel cared for within the relationship. Covenanted sex cannot be casual sex, in other words.

One dimension of covenant is the role of voluntary choice. Although God loves us before we love God, God does not impose love on us; likewise, love and desire are not to be imposed on others. Sexual intimacy, when offered and received as a gift, is a mutually humanizing and satisfying experience. But sexual intimacy becomes an act of violence when pressed upon or taken from another person.

This moral dimension of mutual consent between both partners is a clear example of where the character of the relationship is more important than the form. In the past—and in some settings even today—it has been assumed that a coercive sexual act is valid so long as it takes place between one man and one woman who are married. But clearly the marriage covenant does not confer moral validity on any act of sexual violence.

Likewise, the pursuit of sexual liberty without regard for covenant obligations has often turned out to be a form of abuse and exploitation, rather than an expression of freedom and delight. Whether in the context of marriage or not, when one person's satisfaction of desire is pursued at the expense of another person's humanity and freedom, the hurt and harm that result often extend across many relationships and generations. Such intergenerational harm is illustrated by King David's coercive adultery with Bathsheba, which leads to pregnancy and David's effort to cover up his misconduct by having Bathsheba's husband killed.

This violence is extended through the incestuous rape by David's son Amnon of his sister Tamar and through the violent rebellion of his son Absalom against David's authority, leading to Absalom's death during the civil war that ensues. "The sword will never leave your own house," the prophet Nathan predicts when he describes the consequences of David's sexual abuse (2 Sam. 12:10).

Nathan can be seen as a witness to sexual violence who refuses to be a bystander and who names David's abuse of authority at risk to his own life and status. As people of the covenant, we are called like the prophet Nathan to bear witness to the image of God in all human beings and to challenge sexual coercion and violence wherever it occurs.

At the same time, part of our witness is that God's faithfulness exceeds human failure. The second son born to David and Bathsheba is Solomon, loved by God and blessed with great wisdom—a leader of God's people who builds the magnificent temple and establishes peace.

As can be seen by this story and others like it in the Bible, a key dimension of covenants is that they are fallible. Although God's covenant with God's people is reliable, because of human failure and sin, human covenants are not completely reliable. In other words, people can fail to live up to the obligations of fidelity and mutual care associated with the marriage covenant.

In the biblical tradition, divorce is a legal remedy for the failure of a marriage covenant (Deut. 24:1-4). Divorce revokes the obligations associated with the marriage covenant and leaves former partners free to enter into new marriage covenants—with the exception that they may not enter such a covenant with a former partner from whom they have divorced (Deut. 24:4). Such a return to a former partner is one of many actions that are considered in Leviticus and Deuteronomy to be an abomination to God.

As we saw in chapter four, Jesus' teaching about divorce strengthens the marriage covenant as a protection against infidelity and exploitation and highlights the life-long commitment that is promised in marriage: "what God has joined together, let no one separate" (Matt. 19:3-9). Yet in Matthew's gospel, Jesus does acknowledge the possibility of divorce because of unfaithfulness—as an exception to his general opposition to all divorce (Ewald 64-76).

All of this suggests that covenant relationships should not be taken for granted. We are called in our intimate relationships to honor the covenants we have made and that others have made. When covenants are broken, hearts are also broken, relationships are shattered, households face collapse, and trust is diminished in the broader community.

When we experience broken covenants, our calling as followers of Jesus Christ is to ask for forgiveness when we have contributed to breaking the covenant, to hold partners accountable for dishonoring their covenant obligations, and to seek just reconciliation, even if this reconciliation does not include the repair of the covenant.

When covenant breaking includes the violation of mutual consent or becomes predatory, we must demand accountability and name consequences, even when such accountability threatens the stability of institutions and communities—as it certainly did in the case of King David's crimes. In covenant communities, facing the truth must always take priority over protecting the institution.

Remembering Calling

Finally, we should acknowledge that sexual intimacy is an extraordinary and powerful expression of attachment to another human being. This is why Paul regarded marriage as potentially competing with the demands of Christian discipleship: One who is married can be concerned with the needs of a partner more than with the things of God. At the same time, within the body of Christ, we know that the mutual love and affection expressed in a covenant relationship can display the love of Jesus Christ for the church and be received as a gift of the Spirit that contributes to the mission of the church.

It may be that a believer has chosen to live a celibate life to provide greater freedom for complete devotion to

Jesus Christ and the mission of the church. In such a case, sexual intimacy would of course be experienced as a compromise of calling, even though the church should be able to provide a community of belonging and caring for single people where the humanizing experience of sharing food, friendship, embraces, and other public physical expressions of affection support the call to celibacy.

Even believers who have not chosen celibacy may find the commitments and priorities of a partner or potential partner so divergent from or hostile to the calling of Christ that sexual intimacy will clearly undermine rather than support Christian discipleship. Such a contradictory relationship of intimacy can be described as "unequally yoked" (2 Cor. 6:14 KJV).

It may not always be immediately clear how a specific experience of sexual intimacy will impact faith commitments. In fact, a defining feature of human sexuality is that its expression often exceeds expectations and categories. That is why the wisdom of a discerning community is valuable, even if such a consideration may seem counterintuitive amid the deeply personal feelings aroused by intimacy.

To be sure, sexuality is much broader than sexual intimacy. It is a beautiful and dangerous gift of God, intrinsic to human flourishing and prone to abuse. In sexual intimacy we are able to express deep and vulnerable desires and to give ourselves over to the needs and desires of another. At the same time, the redirection of our erotic desires toward an intense and singular focus on our calling as disciples of Jesus Christ is an even more powerful expression of our most basic humanity.

In either case, the profound delight and extraordinary sorrow associated with sexuality offers us a glimpse of the love and suffering of the God of Jesus Christ—whose passion renews the cosmos and reconciles all things. We pray, therefore, for the life and passion of Jesus Christ to renew our desires and reconcile our lives. Amen.

STUDY QUESTIONS

1. How much authority should we give the church over our personal lives, especially our decisions about sexual intimacy? To what commitments should the church call those of its members who choose to be sexually active?

2. What can we do to hold church members accountable when they engage in sexual abuse and exploitation—including within the context of a marriage relationship?

3. How can we provide support for those who have been hurt by sexual abuse?

4. In what ways might the church help its members think more self-critically and deliberately about the relationship between the Christian calling and the desire for sexual intimacy? What are some examples of choices for sexual intimacy that are excluded from covenant-keeping sexuality?

5. How might the church provide greater support for those who choose singleness as a matter of calling and of household life?

6. How are the experiences of delight and vulnerability that are associated with sexual intimacy brought to mind by the visual illustration at the beginning of this chapter?

7. Does the third figure in the visual illustration at the beginning of this chapter disrupt an otherwise exclusive intimacy? Or does it help to provide a safe space for an honorable and holy relationship? Or is something else going on in this picture?

Appendix A

WAYS TO USE THE STUDY GUIDE

This study guide includes the perspectives of the original five members of the task group as well as clarifying content added by the editors, images created by the illustrator, and additional material reflecting voices within CDC as well as some from beyond. These additional voices were solicited through direct requests for review and input via email and through sample seminars at CDC regional gatherings where participants shared feedback on some excerpts from the guide and sample discussion questions. And yet, these voices are not representative of all in CDC, nor of the wider Mennonite church.

The decision not to include an even wider range of perspectives was a deliberate choice to test an inclusive perspective that increasingly guides CDC leadership decisions at both conference level and congregational levels. This perspective of biblical inclusion and welcome is a view not typically presented in the official statements of Mennonite Church USA and its conferences, nor is it given much attention in books and resources provided by the denominational publishing network. Therefore those who use this study guide should be aware that this guide displays biblical guidance about sexuality from a perspective that challenges the "letter" of current Mennonite teachings about sexuality while seeking to remain true to the deeper "spirit" of these teachings. In CDC we have described this posture as "faithful dissent."

Recognizing that different settings may require different approaches to using the study, we here offer a list of suggested study methods that may help in adapting the content of the study guide to varied contexts. Some of these suggestions incorporate ways to include a wider range of perspectives, and that, too, is intentional. We encourage you to use the study guide in ways that are likely to connect well with the people who make up your congregation, and with the way your congregational life is structured. Not all of these possibilities make sense in all settings. Ignore those that clearly do not fit, but do consider new ways and new groupings of people, so that your conversations may be enriched.

1) *Christian Education*—Elective, adult, young adult, and senior high youth Sunday School classes could review one chapter a week over the course of six weeks. A designated facilitator who commits to guiding the group through the entire book may be helpful in establishing and maintaining trust and comfort within the class.

2) *Small Groups*—Offer the study guide to small groups who are well acquainted and share a more intimate knowledge of one another's lives. They, perhaps, will begin with fewer unwarranted assumptions about one another, which may lead to discussion of greater depth than a group composed of random members of the congregation.

3) *Individuals*—The study guide could be used in daily Bible study on an individual basis. Reading the guide with a Bible close at hand offers an opportunity to meditate on the passages referenced throughout the study guide. The key biblical passages featured in the subheadings of chapters 3 and 4 could organize a more extensive study that made use of Bible commentaries and other study resources.

4) *Youth Groups*—It may seem risky to offer this study

guide to youth, but they are already facing moral questions and choices regarding their own sexuality. This is an opportunity to begin a guided exploration of human sexuality through the wisdom found in the Bible. Grounding their beliefs and understandings in the study of Scriptures, beginning with Genesis and the conviction that human sexuality is a holy and beautiful part of God's creation rather than either a sinful failure or a consumer choice, offers an alternative set of beliefs and understandings from what surrounds them in our culture.

5) *Book Groups*—This study guide offers a view of the Bible through dynamic reading of the Scripture as modeled by Jesus. A book study group could practice dynamic reading of the Scripture together. Begin reviewing and listing some of the differences in perspective in the Bible. Analyze these perspectives represented by so many authors, and consider them in comparison to your own views. A book group could decide to study an introduction to biblical interpretation before discussing this book. An excellent introduction to interpreting the Bible from an Anabaptist perspective is by Perry Yoder, *Toward Understanding the Bible.*

6) *Bible Study Groups*—Use this study guide as a basis to examine the Scriptures included in each chapter. The biblical interpretations offered within each chapter may offer new ways of reading the Scripture passages. Consider your own or your congregation's interpretations and convictions. Note where there is alignment or not, and discuss why.

7) *Worship*—The chapters could be adapted for use in a sermon series. Consider each chapter as a sort of sermon starter, complete with challenging questions to pose to the congregation.

8) *Women's or Men's Groups*—Include this guide as the next series of study in the schedule of Mennonite Women or Mennonite Men gatherings. Consider examining how answers to the study questions may differ when only women's voices are answering as compared to when men's voices are answering or even the voices of a mixed gender group.

9) *Congregational Series of Exploring Human Sexuality in*

Round Table Discussions—To follow the covenant made in the 1980s to continue dialogue about differing experiences and perspectives of sexuality, schedule a series of meetings to provide a place for such discussions to occur. Other resources could be included in such discussions, like the Herald Press *Body and Soul* sexuality curriculum.

10) *Parallel Study*—Print the original CDC human sexuality study group document from here *http://www.mcusacdc. org/human-sexuality/* and study side by side with this study guide. The CDC ministerial committee's document Theological Foundations for Credentialing, printed in Appendix B, could also be included in this study, perhaps as the basis for an additional or concluding study session that focuses on the polity implications of the spiritual and theological direction suggested in the study guide. This exercise might be most appealing to those who enjoy studying source documents.

11) *Perspective Examination*—Study this book in the context of other resources representing a variety of perspectives. Such alternate resources reflecting Mennonite discussions— with generally more conservative or restrictive conclusions—can be found at a webpage curated by Loren Johns entitled "Resources on Homosexuality": *http://ljohns.ambs. edu/glbmenu.htm.*

The resolutions adopted at Saskatoon and Purdue provide an especially helpful summary of the position held by the Mennonite Church USA: *http://ljohns.ambs.edu/Resolutions.htm.* The first section of these resolutions with the theme of "affirmation" could be studied helpfully in relation to chapter 1 of this book.

The second section of the Saskatoon and Purdue resolutions focused on "confession" could be studied usefully in relation to chapter 5 of this book. The third section focused on "covenant" could be discussed helpfully in relation to chapters 2, 3, 4, and 6 of this book.

12) *Mixed Group Study*—Each way of using the study guide contributes a unique, collective perspective that will not be captured in the same way by any other suggested

way of using the study guide. To highlight and to learn from this human reality, consider having two or three groups with different demographics study each chapter.

For example, one group could be a mixed-gender group such as a Sunday School class; another group could be a same- gender group like a women's Bible study. An additional group made up of singles or seniors or some other distinct demographic could also study each chapter.

Schedule a time for members of all the groups to gather together at the same time for reporting from each group about perspectives and focal points that received attention in each group discussion. The differences in points of view that arise can authentically highlight many of the observations made within the study guide about how bodily and cultural experience shapes perspective and understanding.

13) *Comparing Biblical and Scientific Perspectives*—A group of people could supplement the study guide with essays that explore sexuality from various scientific standpoints, such as psychology or biology. This group could compare the biblical understandings displayed in the study guide with scientific knowledge about sexuality, considering points of intersection and tension. Some possible scientific sources include the following essays by Mennonite psychologists and biologists available online:

J. Lamar Freed, Carl S. Keener, and Douglas E. Swartzentruber, "Biological and Psychological Views." In Ruth Conrad Liechty (ed.). *Welcome to Dialogue Series: Mennonites Working to Increase Dialogue on Gay and Lesbian Inclusion.* Retrieved from *http://www.welcome-committee.info/booklet-5-intro.html.*

Carol Lehman. "A Psychologist's Perspective on Same-Sex Orientation." *Mennonite Health Journal* (August 2015). Retrieved from *http://mennohealth.org/mhj_journal/mhj-august-2015/.*

D. J. McFadden. "Biology of Same-Sex Attraction." *Mennonite Health Journal* (August 2015). Retrieved from *http://mennohealth.org/mhj_journal/mhj-august-2015/.*

THEOLOGICAL FOUNDATIONS FOR CREDENTIALING

CENTRAL DISTRICT CONFERENCE MINISTERIAL COMMITTEE
2014

PREFACE

The Ministerial Committee of Central District Conference is providing this statement as our attempt to describe the theological foundations that have informed our work together in recent discussions concerning the credentialing of a man in a committed relationship with another man. We are aware that our recent decisions will be received differently by various individuals and groups within CDC and MC USA. We see this statement as one part of a difficult conversation within the church, and we welcome the response of our Mennonite sisters and brothers as we continue to discern where God is leading us.

STATEMENT

We, the Ministerial Committee of Central District Conference, have been entrusted with the responsibility and privilege of carrying out credentialing processes for the conference. We are guided in this work by our grounding in the biblical story, the theological practices which emerge from the Scriptures and take shape in community, and denominational documents which speak to credentialing matters. Among other qualifications, candidates for credentialing must display a commitment to faith in an Anabaptist perspective, a sense of personal and communal calling, and competency for the tasks of ministry. One of the great blessings of our work is to witness the wide variety of gifts, passions, and testimonies of persons moving toward offices of ministry.

After three decades of official denominational dialogue regarding matters of sexuality and the place of LGBTQ persons within the church body, our committee has received a request from a member congregation to credential a pastor they have called, a gay man. This has raised the larger question of whether we are willing to withhold ministry credentials from an otherwise fully qualified individual solely because of their affectional orientation and their openness to covenanting with a partner with whom to share life.

Our grounding in the biblical story and who we understand and have experienced God to be, have led us to conclude that persons who identify as LGBTQ are not disqualified from ministry credentials because of this one part of who they are. We see in the creation accounts of Genesis a God who delights in the diversity of the cosmos, declaring "good" each new form which arises from the created order. We see in the exodus narrative a God who hears the cries of the oppressed and delivers them out of bondage. We see in the people of Israel and the voice of the prophets the formation of an alternative community based on the practices of covenant faithfulness, mercy and justice. We behold with Isaiah that God does indeed do new things and that it is our task to perceive it when it happens (43:19). We see in Jesus the embodiment of God's good news, much of his life and ministry confronting and challenging religiously held convictions which kept people from embracing their neighbors as fellow children of Abraham (Luke 13:10-17). We see in Saul's conversion a revelation that the very people he believed to be violating God's laws were the very ones God in Christ was claiming as God's own ("Why do you persecute *me*?" Acts 22:7). We identify with Peter's vision in Acts and the overturning of his previous notions of the sacred and the profane ("What God has made clean, you must not call profane." Acts 10:15) We agree with Paul that the Holy Spirit shows up in the form of love, joy, peace, patience, kindness, goodness, gentleness, faithfulness, and self-control (Gal. 5:22-23). We see in the early church glimpses of a new creation, a new humanity, in which biological and social classifications are subsumed within the person of Christ ("There is no longer Jew or Greek, there is no longer slave or free, there is no longer male or female; for all of you are one in Christ Jesus." Galatians 3:28). We do not see in any of the seven biblical passages often referenced as speaking directly to homosexuality any likeness to mutually caring same sex relationships. We hear the call to the ministry of reconciliation as part of the church's mission. (2 Cor. 5:18)

A growing number of congregations within Mennonite Church USA are reading Scripture in this way and are discerning a welcoming posture toward LGBTQ persons for church membership. The Anabaptist value of all baptized believers having and being encouraged to share their ministry gifts makes credentialing of LGBTQ persons who display gifts for pastoral ministry a natural and important next step in realizing this value. While recognizing that we are at a different place in this discernment than the teaching position of Mennonite Church USA, we feel that we are being faithful to our common agreements as members of the same church body. Our Mennonite Polity for Ministerial Leadership notes that "it should not be viewed as a legalistic code; rather, it establishes a trajectory of change which each congregation and conference can follow, as is befitting to their needs and situations" (p. 8). The *Confession of Faith in a Mennonite Perspective* recognizes that it "is subject to the authority of the Bible" and that "confessions give an updated interpretation of belief and practice amid changing times" (p. 8).

Because the Church does not interpret Scripture the same, the Church as a whole is not ready to change these and other foundational documents to be LGBTQ inclusive. Yet we do think there is space within these documents to allow for discernment on the individual, congregational, and conference levels which differs from the majority, and we believe the ground up direction of this movement is often how Spirit-led change has come about in the church throughout history—the ordination of women being a recent example.

In light of all these convictions, if congregations within our conference are ready to call LGBTQ persons as pastors, we are open to using the same credentialing process and holding up the same standards we do for straight candidates. We believe there needs to be a place in the Mennonite church to further test an option besides life-long celibacy for LGBTQ followers of Jesus Christ, even those who feel called to ministry. We are ready to bless and credential qualified candidates no matter their sexual identity, and we welcome the counsel of the pastors and delegates of CDC as we seek to be faithful to the example and call of Jesus Christ and of Scripture.

October 2014

BIBLIOGRAPHY

A Mennonite Polity for Ministerial Leadership. Herald Press, 1996.

Achtemeier, Mark. *The Bible's Yes to Same-Sex Marriage.* 2nd ed. Westminster John Knox Press, 2015.

Bailey, Wilma Ann, and Christina Bucher. *Lamentations, Song of Songs.* Believers Church Bible Commentary. Herald Press, 2015.

Barth, Karl. *Church Dogmatics* III.1. T & T Clark, 1958.

Brownson, James. *Bible, Gender, Sexuality: Reframing the Church's Debate on Same-Sex Relationships.* Eerdmans, 2013.

Cheng, Patrick S. *Radical Love: An Introduction to Queer Theology.* Seabury Books, 2011.

Clemens, Philip K. *Beyond the Law: Living the Sermon on the Mount.* Herald Press, 2007.

Coakley, Sarah. *God, Sexuality, and the Self: An Essay on the Trinity.* Cambridge University Press, 2013.

Confession of Faith in a Mennonite Perspective. Herald Press, 1995.

Enns, Peter. *The Bible Tells Me So: Why Defending Scripture Has Made Us Unable to Read It.* Harper One, 2014.

Ewald, George R. *Jesus and Divorce: A Biblical Guide for Ministry to Divorced Persons.* Herald Press, 1991.

Friesen, Ivan. *Isaiah.* Believers Church Bible Commentary. Herald Press, 2009.

Gerbrandt, Gerald. *Deuteronomy.* Believers Church Bible Commentary. Herald Press, 2015.

Good, Meghan Larissa. "Mirror of God or Idolatry?" *Mennonite World Review* (January 4, 2016), 7.

Grimsrud, Ted and Mark Thiessen Nation. *Reasoning Together: A Conversation on Homosexuality.* Herald Press, 2008.

Gushee, David P. *Changing Our Mind.* 2nd ed. Read the Spirit Books, 2015.

Heggen, Carolyn Holderread. *Sexual Abuse in Christian Homes and Churches.* Herald Press, 1993.

Hershberger, Anne Krabill, ed. *Sexuality: God's Gift.* Herald Press, 2010.

Hanson, Paul. *The Diversity of Scripture: A Theological Interpretation.* Fortress Press, 1982.

Hart, Drew G. I. *Trouble I've Seen: Changing the Way the Church Views Racism.* Herald Press, 2016.

Hubmaier, Balthasar. "Freedom of the Will, I."In H. Wayne Pipkin and John Howard Yoder, trans. and eds., *Balthasar Hubmaier: Theologian of Anabaptism.* Classics of the Radical Reformation, vol. 5. Herald Press, 1989. 426-48.

Hut, Hans, "A Beginning of a True Christian Life." In John Rempel, trans. and ed., *Jörg Maler's Kunstbuch: Writings of the Pilgrim Marpeck Circle.* Classics of the Radical Reformation, vol. 12. Pandora Press, 2010. 115-36.

"Human Sexuality: A Biblical Perspective." Human Sexuality Task Group of Central District Conference, 2015. *http://www.mcusacdc.org/wp-content/uploads/2016/01/Human-Sexuality-Statement-20160217.pdf*

Human Sexuality in the Christian Life. General Conference Mennonite Church and Mennonite Church, 1985. *http://ljohns.ambs.edu/HSCL/hscl-cl.htm*

Instone-Brewer, David. *Divorce and Remarriage in the Church: Biblical Solutions for Pastoral Realities.* Intervarsity Press, 2003.

King, Michael A., ed. *Stumbling Toward a Genuine Conversation on Homosexuality.* Cascadia Publishing House, 2007.

Kraus, C. Norman. *On Being Human: Sexual Orientation and the Image of God.* Wipf and Stock, 2011.

Kraus, C. Norman, ed. *To Continue the Dialogue: Biblical Interpretation and Homosexuality.* Telford, Pa.: Pandora Press U.S., 2001.

Kraybill, Donald B. *The Upside-Down Kingdom.* Herald Press, 2011.

Martin, Dale. *Sex and the Single Savior: Gender and Sexuality in Biblical Interpretation.* Westminster John Knox Press, 2006.

May, Melanie. *A Body Knows: A Theopoetics of Death and Resurrection.* Continuum, 1995.

McCarthy, David Matzko. *Sex and Love in the Home.* London: SCM Press, 2004.

Menno Simons. *The Complete Writings of Menno Simons.* trans., by Leonard Verduin and ed. J. C. Wenger. Herald Press, 1956.

Moxnes, Halvor. *The Economy of the Kingdom: Social Conflict and Economic Relations in Luke's Gospel.* Philadelphia: Fortress Press, 1988.

Nissenen, Martti. *Homoeroticism in the Biblical World: A Historical Perspective.* Fortress Press, 1998.

Pershey, Katherine Willis. A Long Obedience: On Marriage and Other Covenants." *The Christian Century* (Jan. 21, 2015), 20-23.

Roop, Eugene. *Genesis*. Believers Church Bible Commentary. Herald Press, 1987.

Rupp, Mark. "Peace Beyond Welcome." Peace Sunday Sermon, First Mennonite Church, Bluffton. July 3, 2016.

Schlabach, Gerald. "What is Marriage Now? A Pauline Case for Same-Sex Marriage." *The Christian Century* (Oct. 29, 2014), 22-27.

Smith-Christopher, Daniel. *A Biblical Theology of Exile*. Fortress Press, 2002.

Stone, Ken. *Practicing Safer Texts: Food, Sex, and Bible in Queer Perspective*. T&T Clark International, 2005.

Swartley, Willard. *Homosexuality: Biblical Interpretation and Moral Discernment*. Herald Press, 2003.

Thatcher, Adrian, ed. *The Oxford Handbook of Theology, Sexuality, and Gender*. Oxford University Press, 2014.

Toews, John. *Romans*. Believers Church Bible Commentary. Herald Press, 2004.

Trible, Phyllis. *God and the Rhetoric of Sexuality*. Fortress Press, 1978.

Trible, Phyllis. *Texts of Terror*. Fortress Press, 1984,

Wenger, J. C. *Dealing Redemptively with Those Involved in Divorce and Remarriage Problems*. Herald Press, 1965.

Wilson, Brittany E. *Unmanly Men: Refigurations of Masculinity in Luke-Acts*. Oxford University Press, 2015.

Yoder, Perry B. *Toward Understanding the Bible: Hermeneutics for Lay People*. Faith and Life Press, 1978. Also Wipf and Stock, 2006.

Yoder Neufeld, Thomas. *Ephesians*. Believers Church Bible Commentary. Herald Press, 2002.

Zehr, Paul. *1 and 2 Timothy, Titus*. Believers Church Bible Commentary. Herald Press, 2010.

CONTRIBUTORS TO STUDY GUIDE

STUDY GUIDE EDITORS

Carrie A. Mast, First Mennonite Church, Bluffton, Ohio
Gerald J. Mast, First Mennonite Church, Bluffton, Ohio.

HUMAN SEXUALITY TASK FORCE MEMBERS

Loren Johns (Task Group Chair), Eighth Street Mennonite Church, Goshen, Indiana.

Ron Guengerich, Silverwood Mennonite Church, Goshen, Indiana.

Michael Miller, Assembly Mennonite Church, Goshen, Indiana.

Kiva Nice-Webb, Chicago Community Mennonite Church

J. Alexander Sider, First Mennonite Church, Bluffton, Ohio

Regina Shands Stoltzfus, Assembly Mennonite Church, Goshen, Indiana.

ARTWORK AND DESIGN

Alison King, First Mennonite Church, Bluffton, Ohio
Jill Steinmetz, Grace Mennonite Church, Pandora, Ohio

THE EDITORS

Carrie A. Mast assists with the administration of graduate programs in business at Bluffton University and of the Collaborative MBA program shared among Bluffton University, Canadian Mennonite University, Eastern Mennonite University, and Goshen College. Born in Wauseon, Ohio, she graduated from Bluffton with a bachelor of arts in English education (1995) and a master of arts in organizational management (2003). Carrie served in the administration of developmental disability services for Allen County, Ohio, and more recently was the Christian education coordinator at First Mennonite Church in Bluffton. She was appointed to the Central District Conference board of directors as secretary in 2013 and is a member of First Mennonite Church, Bluffton.

Gerald J. Mast teaches communication at Bluffton University and is the author of numerous books and articles including *Go to Church, Change the World: Christian Community as Calling* (Herald, 2012). He was born in Holmes County, Ohio, and received a bachelor of arts in communication from Malone College in 1987. He com-

126 • THE EDITORS

pleted masters (1990) and doctorate (1995) degrees in rhetoric and communication at the University of Pittsburgh. Gerald is the editor of Studies in Anabaptist and Mennonite History and the vice president of the Mennonite Historical Society (Goshen, Ind.). He serves on the missional church committee of Central District Conference and is a member of First Mennonite Church in Bluffton.

When Carrie and Gerald were married in 2008, they formed a blended family that now includes three children: Anna, Jacob, and Jorian. Among their joint projects are a booklet entitled "Teaching Peace to Children with the *Martyrs Mirror*" and a readers theater script focused on the witness of Anabaptist martyr Jacques d'Auchy.